Learning Is in Bloom
Cultivating Outdoor Explorations

. . . .

Ruth Wilson, PhD

Learning Is in Bloom

Cultivating Outdoor Explorations

· · · · · · · · · · · · ·

Ruth Wilson, PhD

Gryphon House
www.gryphonhouse.com

Published by Gryphon House, Inc.
P. O. Box 10, Lewisville, NC 27023
800.638.0928; 877.638.7576 (fax)
Visit us on the web at www.gryphonhouse.com.

"Connecting through Math" and "Let's Find Shapes" by Dr. Gwendolyn Johnson are used with permission.

Library of Congress Cataloging-in-Publication Data
Names: Wilson, Ruth A., 1943-
Title: Learning is in bloom : cultivating outdoor explorations / by Ruth Wilson.
Description: Lewisville, NC : Gryphon House, Inc., [2016] | Includes bibliographical references and index.
Identifiers: LCCN 2015036476 | ISBN 9780876593745
Subjects: LCSH: Nature study. | Outdoor education. | Early childhood education.
Classification: LCC LB1139.5.S35 W549 2016 | DDC 372.21--dc23 LC record available at http://lccn.loc.gov/2015036476

Bulk Purchase
Gryphon House books are available for special premiums and sales promotions as well as for fund-raising use. Special editions or book excerpts also can be created to specifications. For details, contact 800-638-0928.

Disclaimer
Gryphon House, Inc., cannot be held responsible for damage, mishap, or injury incurred during the use of or because of activities in this book. Appropriate and reasonable caution and adult supervision of children involved in activities and corresponding to the age and capability of each child involved are recommended at all times. Do not leave children unattended at any time. Observe safety and caution at all times.

To all the soul-making aspects of nature

Table of Contents

Preface

· ·

This book is about connecting young children with nature, and it provides the what, why, and how of doing so. Readers will find the forty hands-on activities effective in engaging young children in investigating nature, both indoors and outdoors, on the school grounds and on excursions around the neighborhood. While fostering a love of nature is a major goal, the activities also promote all areas of early childhood education and development.

Young children need frequent positive experiences with nature for their holistic development and for becoming environmentally literate individuals. Connecting young children with nature should focus more on fostering a sense of wonder than on teaching facts, more about promoting desired dispositions than on meeting academic benchmarks or achieving standards-based competencies. Yet, the academic areas are not ignored. This book addresses science, math, literacy, and the arts through activities as varied as experimenting with seeds in sand, making a name plate using natural materials, and comparing the size of leaves using informal measurement strategies. This book also offers suggestions on how to include children with special needs and how to deal with children's fears. The guidelines provided help teachers see how to connect children with nature in both developmentally and environmentally appropriate ways. The activities promote empathy, caring, scientific and philosophical inquiry, self-motivation, and independence. Additional topics addressed include nature play, natural play spaces, nature as an integrating context, ecological identity, and environmental literacy.

Acknowledgments

· ·

Many people have contributed directly and indirectly to the development of this book. There's no way to list them all, but I would like to recognize the colleagues with whom I've shared ideas, the friends and family who cheered me on, the students with whom I've worked, and the young children who remind me daily of what it means to live with wonder. To all of you, I am grateful.

I would also like to thank several individuals who contributed directly to this book. Gwendolyn Johnson, math educator at the University of North Texas, developed all the math activities for this book and contributed a discussion on how nature can be used as a resource in promoting mathematical thinking in young children.

Susan Talbott Guiteras, a supervisory wildlife biologist with the U.S. Fish and Wildlife Service, contributed sections of her ecological autobiography.

For these impressive contributions, I am truly grateful. Your tangible contributions and your ongoing support make this book so much more than I could have developed on my own.

Introduction

· ·

My childhood was filled with many rich nature-related experiences. I explored streams, woods, and fields on the farm where we lived. I picked tomatoes, planted peas, and fed the chickens. I made corncob dolls and wooden boats. By the time I became a parent and an educator, not many children were spending their time actively engaged with nature. I found this troublesome.

I taught at Bowling Green State University in Ohio in the 1990s. This was before the terms *biophilia*, *nature deficit disorder*, and *the nature principle* were a part of our mainstream vocabulary and before many people were concerned about the "denaturing" of childhood. I worked with the department of special education, where my primary focus was on preparing teachers to work with young children with special needs.

The integration of young children with special needs into regular education settings was gaining momentum at the time. While the fields of early childhood education and special education were once considered incompatible because of differing philosophies and strategies, new thinking called for an integration of these two disciplines. This new thinking was based on the understanding that a young child with special needs was a young child first and that the disability was just another aspect of the individuality of the child.

This understanding led me to other insights about young children and what they need to thrive. I knew that nature had nurtured me during my childhood years and had motivated me to explore and experiment. I was concerned that, without close connections with nature, children would be missing out on something important to their development and well-being. I decided to make connecting young children with nature an integral part of my professional work.

I worked with the university's environmental studies program to write a grant proposal focusing on nature and young children. I then went about finding ways to integrate early childhood education and environmental education. The concept was difficult for some to grasp. I was frequently asked what I thought early childhood environmental education should teach young children. Some assumed the focus would be on recycling, as sorting materials was something young children could do. Others thought I might try to teach scientific concepts such as the sun being a source of energy and the rainforest as an example of biodiversity. To my delight, I received funding for the project, which launched me onto a whole new path as an educator and writer.

Today, the movement to connect young children with nature continues to grow. We now have some excellent resources and guidelines to help us explain the what and the why of early childhood environmental education. Guidelines, however, aren't enough. We also need the how—and that's what this book is all about. Connecting children with nature includes environmental education, but it's more comprehensive than that. Working to connect children with nature includes the emotional aspects of ecological identity. Open-ended exploration and wondering connect children with nature through positive hands-on experiences.

For young children, nature isn't a topic or subject—it's the world in which they live, learn, and play. It's the milieu or environment in which they can become whole. Becoming whole includes developing an ecological identity that has emotional, spiritual, and aesthetic components. Children's emerging ecological identity allows them to see themselves as a part of the natural world, not separate from it. They also grow in appreciation of nature, not only as a resource to meet our basic survival needs, but also as a wellspring of beauty and wonder that enriches our lives in countless ways.

Young children are curious, inquisitive, imaginative, and eager to learn. Nature is their world, their natural habitat, a place where they can grow in holistic and authentic ways. It is my hope that the ideas and suggestions offered in this book will provide the inspiration and guidance you need to embark on the privilege of immersing children in the wonders of the natural world. The benefits of doing so are far reaching. By strengthening connections between children and nature, you will be fostering their development; promoting love, respect, and appreciation of the natural world; and contributing to the development of a more sustainable and peaceful society.

1

Connecting Children with the Rhythm of Nature

Nature and Children

If we made a list of what children need during their early childhood years, we would certainly include such things as food, shelter, water, and air. We know that young children also need love, security, a sense of belonging, and the freedom to explore. What's sometimes overlooked is children's need for direct contact with nature.

The benefits of connecting children with nature are evident in every area of child development. Nature helps children grow intellectually, emotionally, socially, spiritually, and physically. A review of the professional literature by Andrea Taylor and Frances Kuo indicates that children who spend time in nature are more creative, less stressed, better able to concentrate, physically more active, and interact more positively with others. This same review indicates that time in nature also reduces symptoms of attention deficit disorder, improves problem-solving and observational skills, and fosters a sense of wonder. Additionally, time in nature promotes conservation attitudes and a child's developing ecological identity—the way we see ourselves in relation to the natural world. This is important because how we view our relationship with nature makes a difference in how we act, what we value, and even in our sense of well-being. Most of us know that nature fosters inspiration, enchantment, and a sense of wonder because we've experienced it. While hard to measure, these benefits add to the holistic development of children and their experience of being alive.

When we think of rhythm, we often think of music—primarily in terms of tempo, flow, or pattern—but other aspects of life have rhythm as well. There's a rhythm to our day, to the way we walk and talk, eat and sleep, and even to how our bodies function without much conscious thought. Nature also has a rhythm. We see and feel this in the ebb and flow of tides, the migration of birds and butterflies, seasonal cycles, and the way dawn comes after night. There's a rhythm in the way plants sprout from seeds, gradually mature, and eventually produce more seeds. There's also a rhythm in the way all living things come into this world, grow, and then eventually die. Everything in nature is connected in some way. Helping children become more aware of nature's rhythms and connections will foster their sense of wonder and deepen their interest in the natural world.

In her book *The Sense of Wonder*, Rachel Carson, a highly-respected author and scientist, describes a child's world as "fresh and new and beautiful, full of wonder and excitement." A part of our job in working with young children is to recognize and honor their unique experience of the world. If you watch children as they play and explore, you'll see that they have a rhythm of their own. Children can experience the world as fresh and new and beautiful because their focus is on the here and now—the present moment with all its wonders and possibilities. Adults, on the other hand, tend to get caught up in the pressures of time and the need to get things done. We also have a tendency to take the wonders of nature for granted and to spend very little time just contemplating the expansiveness of the sky or the unfolding of a flower.

Rachel Carson wrote about this concern. "It is our misfortune," she says in *The Sense of Wonder*, "that for most of us that clear-eyed vision, that true instinct for what is beautiful and awe-inspiring, is dimmed and even lost before we reach adulthood." We can help children enjoy their own unique and precious way of knowing the world by moving to their rhythm and trying to see through their eyes.

There's a certain magical thinking in the way young children know the world. We can honor this way of knowing by not contradicting or correcting children when they tell us that a tree can talk or that a stone can think and feel. A child perceiving or imagining the world as being full of wonder reflects an understanding of the essence of things which we, as adults, may no longer recognize. Rachel Carson talks about children's "clear-eyed vision" and their "true instinct" for what is beautiful and awe-inspiring. She urges us, as adults, to "take time to listen and talk about the voices of the earth and what they mean."

When we think of people who are wise, elders probably come to mind more often than young children do; yet, young children can display a great deal of wisdom.

Howard Gardner, author of *Frames of Mind: The Theory of Multiple Intelligences*, suggests existential intelligence as a way of knowing the world. This type of intelligence, he says, leads us to ask questions about the meaning of existence. Even young children ask such questions. You may have heard children ask "Why do people have to die?" "Where did the first seed come from?" or "Can anything be exactly perfect?" You don't have to be concerned about having the right answers to these questions. In fact, it's probably best to not answer the questions at all. Far better, join the child in wondering about the mysteries of life. Wisdom is often expressed in the questions we ask as much as in the answers we give. Following are some suggestions on how to honor and support the wisdom of children:

- Really listen to children, and give them the time and support they need to express their thoughts. Avoid telling them what you think they should be saying or thinking.

- Really talk with children. Children know the difference between being quizzed, redirected, or patronized, and being taken seriously for what they have to offer.

- Encourage wondering questions. You might start by saying something such as, "I sometimes wonder why birds sing. Do they sing because they're happy?" You might then ask, "What do you wonder about?"

- Encourage children to share their ideas in poetic and imaginative expressions. Such expressions might include song, dance, drawings, sculptures, and paintings.

Howard Gardner's theory of multiple intelligences originally suggested seven distinct types of intelligence: logical-mathematical, visual-spatial, musical, interpersonal, intrapersonal, bodily-kinesthetic, and linguistic. In addition to suggesting an existential intelligence, in *Intelligence Reframed: Multiple Intelligences for the 21st Century*, Gardner also proposes the naturalistic intelligence. People with a high naturalistic intelligence tend to be more in tune with nature and are interested in exploring the natural world. They are also more likely to notice patterns and connections in the natural world.

Indications of high naturalistic intelligence in young children include an interest in caring for plants and animals and a tendency to notice similarities and differences in elements of the natural world. They usually enjoy exploring natural areas and collecting materials such as rocks, shells, and seeds.

Everyone has each type of intelligence to varying degrees. Culture, experience, and what children have at birth all play a role in how each type of intelligence develops. For the naturalistic intelligence to flourish, children need frequent, stimulating

experiences with the natural world. We can provide such experiences by giving children opportunities to manipulate and collect a variety of natural materials, encouraging them to closely observe different types of plants and animals, and engaging them in gardening and exploring natural environments.

The term *sustainability* refers to how living systems remain healthy over time. Sustainable systems are critical to the well-being of the entire Earth and every living thing. Connecting children with nature is important for developing an understanding and appreciation of how we all depend on a sustainable natural world for survival. This doesn't mean that we should tell young children to save the Earth. In fact, we should not. Children did not cause the environmental problems we now face, nor are they in a position to "fix it." We do, however, want to plant the seeds of sustainability by helping children care about the environment. Children will care if they become familiar with the wonders of the natural world and understand that Earth is where we live. It is our home.

Connecting children with nature is a win-win situation in that it's good for children and good for Earth. It fosters children's holistic development, and it plants the seeds of understanding and caring for the natural world. Efforts to connect young children with nature are sometimes referred to as *early childhood environmental education* (ECEE). This designation may suggest that connecting children with nature is more about teaching than about experiencing or exploring, more about knowing than feeling, more about stewardship than enjoyment. This is not the case; ECEE is about all of the above.

The North American Association for Environmental Education (NAAEE) defines ECEE as "a holistic concept that encompasses knowledge of the natural world as well as emotions, dispositions, and skills." Following are selected desired outcomes in each of these areas:

- Knowledge
  - Understanding that people depend on the natural world for survival, that the resources for what we eat, drink, breathe, and wear come from nature
  - Awareness that what people do affects nature
  - Awareness that nature is a part of both our local and global environment

- Understanding that everything in nature is interconnected and constantly changing

- Understanding that all living things have basic survival needs

- Emotions

  - Sense of wonder

  - Enjoyment of the aesthetic and sensory aspects of nature

  - Sense of excitement and inventiveness while exploring the natural world

  - Dispositions

  - Intellectual curiosity about nature

  - Seeing oneself as a part of nature

  - Sensitivity to the beauty and diversity of the natural world

  - Self-motivation to explore the natural world

  - Sense of caring and respect for nature

  - Willingness to actively explore the natural world

- Skills

  - Observing—using the senses to gather information

  - Comparing—identifying similarities and differences in different aspects of the natural world

  - Classifying—grouping and sorting natural objects and phenomena according to properties

  - Measuring—making quantitative descriptions of natural objects and phenomena

  - Communicating—conveying ideas and descriptions orally, in written form such as words or drawings, and/or in three-dimensional representations such as sculptures

- Inferring—making judgments about the natural world based on observation; finding more meaning from a situation than can be directly observed

- Predicting—making reasonable guesses about the ways of the natural world based on observation, prior knowledge, and experience

The Current Disconnect

Perhaps we were fortunate enough to have known the world as a place of wonder during our own childhood years because we had opportunities to explore a nearby wood, watch hummingbirds and butterflies move from flower to flower in our backyards, and pick tomatoes or dig carrots in our families' gardens. Unfortunately, such opportunities are far less available to children today than they were for children of previous generations. This is due, in part, to the loss of access to natural areas in our neighborhoods and to the increase in the amount of time adults and children spend engaged with electronic media. The results are quite troubling.

Richard Louv, in his widely popular book *The Last Child in the Woods*, introduces the phrase *nature deficit disorder* as a description of the human costs of separation from

nature. These costs are especially noticeable in children and can include academic, developmental, and behavioral concerns. A growing body of research, as reported by Louv in his book, indicates that children's separation from nature contributes to attention difficulties, diminished use of the senses, obesity, depression, and higher rates of physical and emotional illnesses.

Separation from nature also interferes with developing an understanding of and love for the natural world. For children and adults alike, this can become a barrier to a healthy ecological identity and a commitment to caring for the environment.

Some children growing up without close connections with the natural environment also develop unfounded fears and prejudices against the world of nature. For some, this takes the form of not wanting to get dirty or wet or cold. For others, this means being afraid of living things such as white-tailed deer and butterflies. Unfounded fears and prejudices against nature are real barriers to understanding and appreciating the natural environment. In fact, fears and prejudices can lead to violence against nature and may be expressed in such actions as killing harmless snakes and trying to eradicate bees from a yard.

Several years ago, a group of four- and five-year-olds were interviewed to get an idea of what they thought and how they felt about nature. These interviews were conducted individually so that their responses would not influence each other. Following are some of the questions and typical answers from these interviews. In analyzing the children's responses, it's important to consider the age of the children and that what they say may not be what they would necessarily do. Some expressions of violence, for example, may reflect fear of the unfamiliar rather than a desire to harm.

Question: **Where could you find wildlife?**

Answers:

At the zoo

In the rainforest

I don't know.

Question: **What would you do if you were close to a butterfly?**

Answers:

Catch it

Hold it in my hand

Put it in a jar

Kill it

Smash it

Question: **Do you like wolves?**

Answers:

No, they would kill you.

They huff and puff and blow your house down.

They're mean.

Question: **Where do you think we should put our trash?**

Answers:

At the end of the street

In the trash can

I don't know.

Question: **Do you think you should help save the Earth?**

Answers:

My dad said we should recycle.

I guess so.

I don't even know what the Earth is.

Many more children now live in urban areas than at any other time in our history. Until recently, many urban planners gave little thought to the need for children's access to nearby nature. While some children living in urban areas have access to city parks, these play areas often include more concrete and equipment than nature. The result is that many children today have very limited opportunities for direct experiences with the natural world.

"Will there still be snow when I grow up?" "Why can't we swim in the lake?" "Do all animals live in the zoo?" These real questions asked by children indicate that our world is changing in dramatic ways and that children today are growing up in a world far more toxic and unstable than any other generation has experienced. We're now faced with an alarming extinction of species; but for children, there's also an extinction of experience.

Robert Michael Pyle, author and internationally known expert on butterflies, first introduced the term *extinction of experience* in his book *The Thunder Tree*. Pyle was referring primarily to how the loss of species in our own neighborhoods lessens our experience of nature. Once elements of nature disappear from our own personal world, our sense of connections to the natural world is also diminished. This is true for many children today and, as a result, holistic child development and the future of our natural world are at risk. The extinction of experience, Pyle explains, will ultimately lead to a lack of concern for the world of nature. This, in turn, will lead to further destruction of the natural world.

There's certainly little doubt that the introduction of television, computers, and video games into children's lives has greatly reduced the amount of time children spend outdoors. While data vary on the amount of time preschoolers spend with electronic media, there's little doubt that screen time is replacing time outdoors for many children. The result is a troubling divide between children and the world of nature. Screen time itself isn't necessarily harmful for children. The concern is about the misuse and overuse of technology. What we should strive for is a healthy balance between screen time and more hands-on nature-related activities. This balance, unfortunately, seems to be moving in an unhealthy direction.

Children's Rights

Children have basic rights, including the right to live and play in an environment that stimulates their healthy development. These rights are spelled out in a document adopted by the United Nations General Assembly in 1989, the *Convention on the Rights of the Child* (CRC). The United States and Somalia are the only two countries in the UN that have not yet ratified this important international agreement.

The CRC lists the universally accepted rights for children and calls on all nations to protect and enhance these basic rights through their policies, programs, and services. Some of the basic rights included are the right to freedom of expression, the right to be protected from exploitation, and the right to an education. As expressed in the CRC, the education of the child should include helping children develop to their fullest potential and develop respect for the natural environment. The CRC also includes a statement about children's right to play.

Within the last several years, there has been a growing recognition of another basic right that some are saying should be added to the CRC: the right of children to connect with nature. The International Union for the Conservation of Nature is one organization promoting official recognition of this basic right. Their argument is based on a concern about the increasing disconnect between children and nature and the adverse consequences for both healthy child development and responsible stewardship for the natural world. Responsible stewardship is the only way to protect another basic right of children: their right to a healthy future.

Guidelines and Resources

Since the early 1990s, there have been dramatic developments in integrating early childhood education and environmental education. We now have a set of professional guidelines, published by the NAAEE, and multiple resources to guide our efforts in connecting young children with nature in developmentally appropriate ways.

The following suggestions for early childhood environmental education are based on the unique characteristics and needs of young children and are designed for anyone working directly with children in a variety of settings.

- **Provide frequent, positive experiences in natural environments.** Children's time in nature should be on a daily or almost daily basis and should allow for hands-on exploration. Children learn about nature by interacting with nature, not by hearing about it or watching TV documentaries.

- **Focus on experiencing versus teaching.** While outdoors, it's far better to let children explore and play rather than attend to lessons you may be trying to teach. Children will learn from observing, listening, feeling, pouring, digging, and experimenting. Hands-on experiences with nature have far more teaching power than prepared lessons have.

- **Respect children's fears and follow their interests.** Not all children come to nature with the same background and interests. Some children will be fearful of things they are not familiar with. Others may have been taught that some things in nature can hurt them. These fears should be respected. While a gradual introduction to things they are fearful of can diminish or eliminate children's fears, the process should not be forced. Encourage children's interests, even if what children choose to focus on is of little interest to you or relates to what is unfamiliar to you. For example, a child might be drawn to different kinds of rocks. He especially likes to experiment with how some rocks shatter or crack when hit with another rock. You may not be familiar with the different kinds of rocks and may even feel that pounding rocks has little educational value. You can still support the child's interest by encouraging him to describe what he's doing and discovering and by really listening to what he says. You can also encourage him to share his findings with others, perhaps through displays, drawings, and so on. Be attentive to any questions the child might have about rocks, and help him find answers to his questions.

- **Model interest in and caring for the natural environment.** Young children learn from nature by interacting with it—no direct teaching needed. We have a role to play, however, in helping children learn to relate to nature in respectful and caring ways. Many children enjoy looking for and catching a variety of critters. They delight in find-ing bugs under rocks or logs and netting minnows and tadpoles from streams and ponds. An important lesson for children to learn from these activities is that living creatures should be treated with respect. If we catch a critter, we should return it to its home after we've had a chance to observe it for a short period of time.

- **Avoid telling young children to save the Earth.** While we want chil-dren to love nature and respect the Earth, saving an environment in crisis is not a burden we should put on young children. Asking children to save the Earth is, in a sense, asking them to fix something they did not break and to handle something they are not equipped to handle. Even giving children messages about an endangered Earth can have the

opposite effect from what we are trying to accomplish in connecting children with nature. The idea of our planet in danger can instill fear and feelings of helplessness in young children. These feelings actually work against developing a positive relationship with nature.

• **Be sensitive to different family priorities and views about the natural world and our interactions with it.** One of the best ways to identify the traditions and perspectives of children and their families is to get to know them on a personal level. Invite their ideas about how to include their cultural priorities and goals in your program and activities. It's also important to consider the family's view of nature-related activities for their children. If you know that parents consider worms and bugs off-limits, you should avoid pressuring the child to hold the critters in her hand. You can, however, still foster the child's positive connections with nature by encouraging close observation and helping her understand that all living creatures contribute in some way to the functioning of the whole.

• **Provide child-friendly tools to encourage closer observation and hands-on manipulation of natural materials.** Magnifying glasses are an obvious example of a tool that can be used for closer observation, but many other tools encourage children to look more closely. These include hand-held, nonbreakable mirrors; drop cloths to catch things that fall from trees and bushes; insect-observation containers; clipboards and paper for recording observations; field binoculars; plant and animal identification cards; flashlights; specimen boxes; pretend cameras; and empty picture frames. A picture frame with the backing and glass removed can be used to mark off an inspection area on the ground. Children will be amazed by how many different stones, creatures, and plants can be found inside that small area. Children can also hold the frame up to frame a picture of something in nature. At a later time, a child may choose to describe or even draw what she captured in the frame. Use questions to invite closer observation: How tall is this plant? Which weighs more—a cup of water or a cup of sand? How far from the tree did the wind blow these seeds? Tools that encourage hands-on manipulation of natural materials include any type of digging tool, rakes, buckets, sifters, sorting trays, plastic cups, and child-size wheelbarrows and wagons.

- **Focus on open-ended activities.** An open-ended activity is an activity that allows for a great deal of freedom in how it is conducted. Stirring found materials such as leaves and flower petals in a bucket of water is an example of an open-ended activity. Coloring a predrawn image of a leaf is an example of a closed activity. Open-ended activities invite imagination and creativity and, at times, require problem-solving skills and persistence.

- **Give children plenty of opportunities to choose their own activities.** Allowing children to choose their own activities is consistent with differing interests and abilities and reflects an understanding of how different children march to different rhythms.

- **Keep it simple and keep it local.** Children don't need a half-acre garden to learn that much of what we eat comes from plants. A little lettuce or a few carrots grown along a fence can give young children rich opportunities for planting, harvesting, and tasting. A single tree in the yard can be almost as instructive as an entire forest for learning concepts related to the seasons or observing how other living things depend on trees for shelter. Keeping it simple also means getting children engaged with nature right outside the door rather than depending on field trips for nature-related experiences. It's important for children to connect with their own place, to become familiar with the unique sights, sounds, smells, and cycles of their immediate environment. Young children can start by walking barefoot in the grass or sand or by burying themselves in a pile of leaves.

Keep It Local

Gardening with children is one way to help them learn about some of the unique characteristics of the place where they live. Gardening requires attention to local weather and climate and an awareness of wildlife in the area that might interfere with growing and harvesting food. Once the food is harvested, children can learn important lessons about reaching out to others in the community by sharing some of what they've grown.

Primary Objective

Children will become more aware of some of the characteristics of their local natural environment. They will also become actively engaged with other people in their community.

Materials

Gardening tools
Planting containers or beds
Potting soil
Seeds or seedlings of fruits and vegetables that will grow in your area
Watering cans or hoses

What You Can Do

1. Identify a suitable place for gardening. You can use raised beds, containers, or ground plots. The important thing is to have good soil and enough light. Talk to the children about what makes a good place for plants to grow well and what time of the year they grow.

2. Choose suitable plants for the local environment. Talk to the children about how some of the food we eat, such as bananas and pineapples, may come from faraway places, while other food is grown closer to where they live. In gardening with children, it's best to choose plants that are easy to grow, have short growing seasons, and are fun to harvest. Plants that work well in many

temperate climates include lettuce, radishes, snow peas, cherry tomatoes, carrots, and potatoes. It's always fun to include some flowers, such as sunflowers, petunias, and zinnias.

3. Involve the children in planting, watering, and harvesting the garden. Encourage them to taste some of the food they grow.

4. Share some of the produce with a local food pantry and some of the flowers with a nursing home.

Additional Suggestions

- Take a field trip to a local farm or farmer's market, and talk with the farmers about what crops are locally grown and how they grow their crops.

- Keep a log about weather and growth patterns during the growing season.

- Check out the ideas and resources at the Kids Gardening website, http://www.kidsgardening.org.

Since 1998, early childhood educators from countries around the world have been meeting to share ideas about services for young children in diverse settings. This group, the World Forum Foundation, has been discussing the importance of nature in the lives of young children. Several years ago, they established the Nature Action Collaborative for Children (NACC) and developed a set of universal principles for connecting children with nature. These universal principles are targeted at four different groups: children, design professionals, educators, and families. The principles state that it is important for educators to:

- allow enough time each day for children to explore freely in nature-based spaces;

- understand their role as researchers and facilitators who observe children's interactions with nature and support the emergent curriculum;

- support children's appropriate risk taking and adventurous play in nature;

- provide children with opportunities for silence and contemplation in natural settings; and

- encourage children's development of a sense of wonder and a sense of environmental stewardship.

The entire set of principles for connecting children with nature can be accessed at http://www.worldforumfoundation.org/wf/nacc/ibm/pdf/universal_princ_dvd_english.pdf.

There are many resources available for connecting children with nature. An important consideration in choosing which ones to use in an early childhood setting is the issue of developmental appropriateness. Hopefully, the above guidelines and the resources listed on page 181 will help you decide how to strengthen the bonds between young children and the world of nature. The resources focus primarily on organizations and publications developed by those organizations. There are certainly many other excellent resources, such as books, websites, and companies, for connecting children with nature.

Current Initiatives

Efforts to connect children with nature can take many different forms and be offered in a variety of settings. Some of these efforts focus on what families can do together in community outings or what parents can do at home to provide more nature-related experiences for their children. To support these efforts, the Children and Nature Network has instituted a Natural Family Network, which supports establishing nature clubs for families. This is an excellent resource for getting families on board in connecting children with nature.

Other current initiatives for connecting children with nature take the form of educational programs for groups of children. These include nature preschools and forest kindergartens. A nature preschool is an early childhood education program that uses nature as an integrating context or central focus of its curriculum. Children in a nature preschool typically go outside for an extended period of time every day with many opportunities for playing and exploring in a natural area. Indoors, every area and activity is infused in some way with nature.

Children in forest kindergartens, or forest schools, typically spend their entire school day outdoors. These programs are usually designed for young children ages three to six and focus specifically on strengthening children's bond with nature. Some programs operate entirely without a building. While forest schools are more popular in some European countries, they are gaining popularity in the United States.

Two other current initiatives in connecting young children with nature include the development of natural play spaces and the nature play movement. Following is a brief description of each with much more discussion provided in Chapter 2. Natural play spaces, also called environmental yards, are outdoor areas intentionally designed to integrate natural components into a place for play and learning. Some natural play spaces take the form of a children's garden where gardening with children and/or play in a garden setting may be emphasized. The Natural Learning Initiative associated with North Carolina State University is a primary source of information on the what, why, and how of natural play spaces.

Nature play is a movement to take children back to what once was the natural way to play. There was a time before playground equipment, video games, and battery-operated toys, when children climbed trees, made mud pies, floated toy bark boats down rivers and streams, and played with corncob dolls. Children in these earlier times engaged in nature play, which can take place indoors as well as outdoors and comes naturally to children when they are given the time, freedom, and materials to become actively engaged with the natural world.

Another recent initiative focusing on connecting young children with nature is the development of college-level teacher-education courses and certificates. Antioch University New England, for example, now offers a nature-based early childhood specialization within the elementary education certification program. They also offer a nature preschool/forest kindergarten professional development program designed to train teachers, administrators, and founders of nature preschools and forest kindergartens. Morton College in Illinois and Florida Atlantic University also offer coursework in early childhood environmental education. The Morton College program, developed in collaboration with Brookfield Zoo and the Chicago Zoological Society, can lead to an early childhood nature play certificate. Florida Atlantic University offers three courses in early childhood environmental education. In addition to providing a comprehensive view of ECEE, this coursework also engages students in exploring local natural habitats for firsthand learning and content experience.

Connecting through Intentionality

To be intentional is to make decisions and act with a purpose in mind. Being intentional as a teacher means knowing what you want for the children and then arranging the environment, planning activities, and interacting with the children in a way that promotes the goals you've identified.

A basic belief in early childhood education is that children learn best through self-selected activities, that they should be free to explore and manipulate materials on their own terms. The understanding is that children will gain knowledge and acquire skills through their own child-guided experiences. This is true for many early childhood milestones, but intentional teaching with some teacher-directed activities also plays a critical role in helping children reach desired goals.

As we work with young children, we should foster an interest in and respect for the world of nature. Working toward this goal will, in most cases, involve a healthy balance of child-directed and teacher-directed activities. Connecting children with nature means going beyond developing a specific lesson plan or activity. It involves keeping connections with nature in mind as you prepare the environment, interact with children, and communicate with parents. It's realizing and acting on the understanding that nature should be an ongoing part of a young child's life and that it can be integrated into every aspect of the curriculum.

Making nature a focus of the curriculum also goes beyond teaching children facts about nature. For some teachers, this can be a bit confusing. They may wonder whether they should focus on education or enchantment. They may wonder whether we want children to develop attitudes and values related to good stewardship of the environment or do we want their time in nature to be focused on fostering creativity and experiencing joy? Fortunately, nature has what's needed to accomplish all of the above. When it comes to education or enchantment, we can choose both.

Nature offers beauty, diversity, and interconnectedness. Nature also offers surprises and opportunities for challenge. Immersed in nature, we often experience awe and a sense of wonder. At times, we may even experience a sense of oneness with the universe. Such experiences—even in young children—tend to foster one's imagination and creativity. They also invite reflection and philosophical thinking and support the spiritual life of children.

Nature is a powerful motivating force as it invites observation, exploration, and experimentation. Children tend to ask a lot of what, why, where, and how questions as they explore and play freely outdoors. What is that sticky stuff on the tree? Why do the bees buzz around the purple flowers? Where do the butterflies go at night? How do the birds make their nests? Even if we don't know all the answers to the questions children ask, the very act of questioning often leads to new understandings about the world of nature and develops skills needed for self-directed learning. Such questioning can also lead to an appreciation of the awesomeness of nature.

In many instances, as children interact with the natural world, it's nature that will do the teaching. Shakespeare once wrote that there are "tongues in trees, books in the running brooks, sermons in stones, and good in everything." One of our privileges as teachers of young children is to help them hear the stories and sermons that nature has to share.

On their website, the Environmental Education Council of Ohio defines *environmental education* as "education in, for, and about the environment." One of the primary goals is the development of environmental literacy, which includes understanding the natural world and our relationship with it. At the early childhood level, the extent of this understanding will differ dramatically from what might be expected of older children and adults, yet promoting environmental literacy should be a part of every early childhood education program.

When we look at the historical roots of early childhood education, we see some overlaps with environmental education. Both Maria Montessori, founder of the Montessori approach, and Freidrich Froebel, the founder of kindergarten, for example, stressed the importance of children spending time in nature. They believed that time in nature would promote children's holistic development and help them learn. Today, we're beginning to understand the importance of starting early in helping children care for the environment as well. In terms of what is good for children and the environment, we may wish to add another descriptor to how we define environmental education: learning from the environment. Doing so may be a way to more fully engage the hearts and souls of children in caring for the environment.

Education from the environment touches us at the emotional level and teaches us lessons about how we might live in harmony with the world of nature. Learning from the environment helps us tap into wisdom, intuition, and other ways of knowing. With nature as our teacher, we learn about interdependence, diversity, beauty, mystery, life, death, adaptation, interconnectedness, patterns, and cycles. We also learn important lessons about who we are—a part of something much bigger than ourselves.

Most early childhood educators are committed to promoting the development of the whole child versus focusing exclusively on academic learning or cognitive development. One area of holistic development that has not received much

attention, however, is the ecological self or ecological identity. The ecological self is an individual's connections with and attitudes toward the natural environment. This aspect of who we are—while always present—can expand and mature over time.

A number of factors influence how a child's ecological self will develop: where the child lives and plays, cultural priorities and values, and educational experiences. Perhaps the most important factor in developing a healthy ecological self is the opportunity for frequent positive experiences with the natural world.

Writing an ecological autobiography, the story of one's life in relation to the natural world, is one way to gain a deeper understanding of your ecological self and how this aspect developed over time. A well-written ecological autobiography includes not only what you did and experienced in nature but also the feelings and insights gained through such experiences. Susan Talbott Guiteras was a senior in college when she wrote her ecological autobiography. As she wrote, Susan was able to identify four different stages in the development of her ecological identity from early childhood through young adulthood:

- Nature, My Playground

- Nature, My Classroom

- Nature, My Responsibility

- Nature, My Friend

About fifteen years after completing her ecological autobiography, Susan added a new section, Nature, My Career, in which she described some of her experiences and insights working as a wildlife biologist.

Following are some excerpts from Susan's ecological autobiography representing the different stages in her development.

Nature, My Playground

There were several children my age in the neighborhood, and they all shared with me the love of playing in the woods, hunting critters, and getting dirty. . . . [We had] the freedom to roam and conduct our activities without parents around. . . . We used to meet inside a circle of pine trees near the edge of the park. The ground there was a soft, thick layer of brown pine needles that gave the look of carpeting and the trees blocked just enough light to give it an enclosed and sacred feeling. We called it The Tree Circle, and it was the site of many playful gatherings.

Nature, My Classroom

Salamanders represent a transition in my relationship with nature . . . . We found them on our own! . . . If we were to be successful hunters, we had to recognize rocks and logs with salamander potential. . . . There were many different teachers along the way, few of them human and some of them not living at all. . . . We used to collect frog eggs every spring and keep them in aquariums. They would hatch, and the tadpoles would feed and grow and eventually develop legs and lose their tails. That was an incredible lesson in the wonders of metamorphosis!

Nature, My Responsibility

As I got older and learned more about the outdoors, I began to develop feelings toward nature that went beyond simple enjoyment and fascination. The first teacher to present to me a lesson in responsibility for the natural world was Penny, a young snapping turtle . . . . Ignorant to the future consequences, I decided that this creature would make a wonderful pet. . . . I kept Penny in various fish bowls and aquariums throughout her years with me. . . . Learning to care for Penny was, of course, a lesson in the sense that I was still learning from nature. . . . As I got older, I realized that Penny was my responsibility—that I had altered her natural life and was therefore responsible for making the best of it. . . . Caring for Penny over a decade taught me the importance of taking responsibility for the ways in which I disrupt the natural world.

Nature, My Friend

My relationship with nature has grown and deepened in much the same way that a strong, lasting friendship between two people can evolve. I have reached the point now where I can honestly say that I see Nature as a close friend. We have played together, I have learned from Nature, and I feel a responsibility toward helping Nature thrive. As I prepare to move forward with life after college, it has occurred to me that Nature is such an important friend that I will not settle in a place where I cannot be near it. Someday I will probably have a child or two, and I cannot wait to introduce them to my friend.

Nature, My Career

Nature is my career now, just as I had hoped, and just as my parents had probably predicted when I was a small child . . . As a naturalist, I was able to see firsthand what natural and easy friends children and Nature can be. There seems to be some instant respect between the two. . . . I am married, and we hope to start a family in the near future. And I suppose that is when the full circle of my relationship with nature can begin again in a new way. I can't wait!

Rhythm in Our Work with Children

Young children and nature have several things in common. Both do better when nurtured in healthy environments, both are full of surprises, and both bring joy. Another thing young children and nature have in common is a rhythm of their own. Both do better when this rhythm is recognized and respected. Forcing them to hurry to maturity works against their best interests.

We do our finest work as early childhood educators when we match the rhythm of the day and year to the rhythm of the young children in our care. At times, this means entering into the enthusiastic explorations of children as they dig for dinosaur bones in the yard or blow bubbles outdoors on a windy day. At other times, this means pausing long enough to watch a hummingbird hover near a bush or wait patiently as a child finishes a chalk drawing of a flower on the sidewalk.

The rewards of matching our rhythm to the rhythm of young children include seeing them grow and blossom in remarkable ways. Physical growth of children over time is obvious. How they grow in other ways—emotionally, spiritually, socially, and ecologically—is often subtler but ever so critical to their holistic development. Connecting children to nature is one avenue that should not be overlooked in our efforts to help them become all that they can be.

We might look to the words of the poet Walt Whitman for further assurance about the effect of nature on the lives of young children.

> There was a child went forth every day;
> And the first object he look'd upon, that object he became;
> And that object became part of him for the day, or a certain part of
>   the day, or for many years, or stretching cycles of years.
> The early lilacs became part of this child,
> And grass, and white and red morning-glories, and white and red
>   clover, and the song of the phoebe-bird,
> And the Third-month lambs, and the sow's pink-faint litter, and
>   the mare's foal, and the cow's calf,
> And the noisy brood of the barn-yard, or by the mire of the pond-side,
> And the fish suspending themselves so curiously below there—and
>   the beautiful curious liquid,
> And the water-plants with their graceful flat heads—all became
>   part of him.

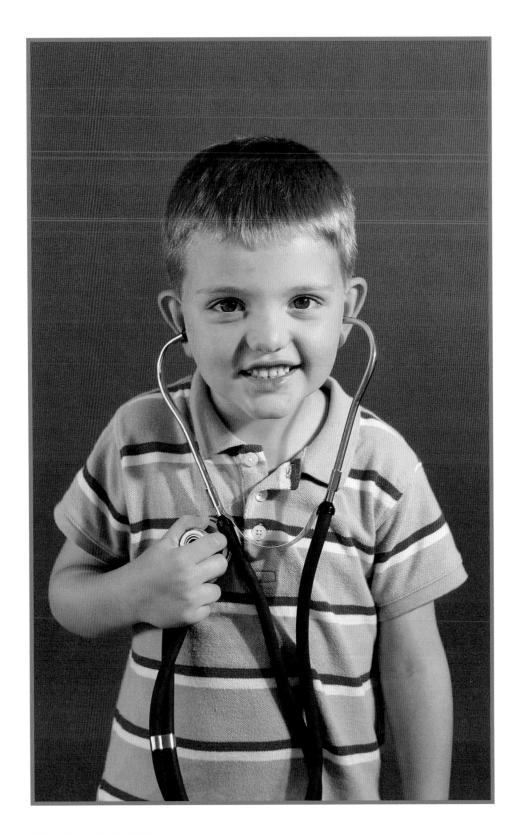

2

Connecting
through Play

. . . .

Play and Active Learning

A recent discussion among a grandmother, mother, and grandchild focused on plans for a Saturday afternoon. "My job this afternoon," said the grandmother, "is to get some groceries and then do the laundry." "I have to clean the house," announced the mother. "And what is your job?" Grandmother asked four-year-old Kya. Without hesitation, Kya responded by saying, "My job is to play."

And Kya was right—her job was to play. As early childhood educators, we sometimes repeat what Maria Montessori so clearly articulated: "Play is the work of the child." In their book *Play and Child Development*, Joe Frost, Sue Wortham, and Stuart Reifel note how play fosters the development of young children in the areas of fine and gross motor skills, language, socialization, emotional well-being, an understanding of self and others, problem solving, and creativity. Play also stimulates brain development and enhances a child's learning ability.

According to Montessori and most other early childhood experts, true play is voluntary, enjoyable, purposeful, and spontaneous. It's also an active process, engaging the body, mind, and spirit of the child. Close observation of children at play indicates that while they're playing they are often engaged in solving problems, expanding on new ideas, and figuring out how to deal with a variety of social and emotional challenges. Through play, children are also learning basic concepts relating to such things as cause and effect, gravity, balance, height, weight, light, sound, as well as the characteristics and behaviors of living things. We can try to teach these basic concepts to children, but true understanding comes through self-discovery usually arrived at through play.

Play takes different forms. It can be solitary or social; play can focus on constructing or pretending.

The following are some categories of play:

- Exploratory—Children explore the properties and functions of different materials, equipment, and objects. They explore the way certain materials are alike and different, how something works, and what they can do with different materials and objects. This type of play can include experimentation, trial and error, and cause-and-effect explorations.

- Dramatic—Children take on roles or pretend to be someone or something else that is familiar to them. They may pretend to be a person, such as a parent, camper, gardener, or doctor; an animal, such as a dog, bird, snake, or horse; or a thing, such as a tree, machine, or door. This type of play can be played alone or with others. One of the special benefits of pretending to be an animal is the way it can help young children become more sensitive to the needs and characteristics of that animal.

- Fantasy—Children create costumes or props and use these as they engage in imaginative adventures. Fantasy play often includes taking on the role of an imagined character, such as a fairy, a monster, a superhero, or a wizard.

- Constructive—Children manipulate materials and objects to build things. Constructive play is often exploratory in nature as children try out different materials and methods to see what they can make. With blocks, they build towers; with wet sand, they make castles; with sticks, they build shelters.

- Physical—Children engage in large-muscle movements, such as running, jumping, throwing, kicking, dancing, and climbing. At times, physical play involves combining movements, as when running while throwing or kicking a ball. Of course, the other types of play often involve physical activity, as well.

- Games with rules—Children follow or create rules as they play. Games with rules include board games such as Candy Land and physically active games such as tag, hide and seek, and soccer. Children often set rules during dramatic play, as well. These rules involve barking like a dog if you're a dog character or crying like a baby if you're a baby character.

Children, of course, don't refer to these different categories when asked what they like to do when they play. What children talk about is the importance of having fun, being with friends, choosing freely, and being outside. Children under the age of three usually prefer slightly different play activities than older children. Infants enjoy exploring their immediate environment with a nurturing adult close by. Infants and toddlers also prefer small-scale spaces rather than wide-open spaces. While outdoors, they especially like access to a variety of things on the ground that respond to their explorations. They enjoy sand, leaves, dirt, and grass as these are materials they can hold, pick, tear, and pour.

Preschool- and kindergarten-age children enjoy constructing things, especially when they have a variety of open-ended materials to work with. They like transporting materials and creating small spaces. They also enjoy engaging in "real" work, using real tools such as shovels, wheelbarrows, and rakes.

Anyone who has ever worked with children knows that not all play is equal. Where children play, what they play with, and the central focus of their play affect the quality of their play. Natural environments and natural materials are especially conducive to rich play experiences for young children.

Nature Play

Nature play involves active engagement with nature. This type of play often occurs outdoors in a natural area but can also occur indoors using natural materials. While nature play was common for children growing up in earlier times, opportunities for this type of play have greatly diminished as families move from rural to urban and suburban neighborhoods and as streams, woods, and vacant lots have disappeared from the lives of children.

Additionally, children today are more likely to be watching television and playing computer games than exploring natural areas and playing with natural materials. This "de-naturing" of play can lead to alienation from the natural world. Concerned parents, educators, and other professionals are calling for a return to nature play in the lives of young children. This concern has led to the development of environmental yards or natural play spaces, using natural materials for play props, and encouraging children to spend more time outdoors.

Sand, soil, and sticks are examples of natural materials that make wonderful play props and are essential for nature-play activities. Children find many creative ways to play with natural materials, both indoors and out. Natural materials can be easily manipulated and are rich in transformability and flexibility. An ice cube can become a puddle of water; dry leaves can be crushed and become "nature's confetti." A stick can become a spoon for stirring soup or a tool for writing in the sand. Children readily use natural materials for building, for "cooking," for making collages or designs, for pouring and stacking, for burying, for transporting, and for many other imaginative activities.

Mini Gardens and Mini Forests

Combining natural materials with a few other props can lead to interesting creations. Some great props for fostering creativity and encouraging exploration include spray bottles filled with water; digging tools; containers such as egg cartons, shoe boxes, and small plastic bottles; cooking utensils; and playdough. While children will find many ways on their own to use these props, you can also provide a few suggestions. One idea is to use playdough as a base for creating mini gardens and mini forests.

Primary Objective

Children will explore the characteristics of natural materials by creating mini gardens or mini forests.

Materials

Natural materials, such as sticks, pebbles, seeds, and leaves
Playdough
Trays or shoe-box lids

What You Can Do

1. Spread some playdough on a tray or shoe-box lid or directly on a table top.

2. Collect small pieces of natural materials, such as short sticks, pebbles, seeds, and leaves.

3. Encourage the children to make a mini garden or mini forest by pushing the natural materials into the playdough.

Additional Suggestions

- Use natural materials, such as a pine twig, for painting.

- Make prints using pinecones, seed pods, or acorn caps.

- Fingerpaint with mud.

- Use natural materials for "cooking." Provide pots and pans, spoons, spatulas, and plates. Have soil, sand, water, and a variety of plant parts available.

- Provide props for "camping": sheet for a tent, camp stool, sticks for a pretend camp fire and for roasting marshmallows, and so on.

- Provide props for gardening—wheel barrow, digging tools, straw hat, watering can, and so on.

- Provide props for a farmers' market—tables, a variety of fruits and vegetables (preferably real and grown by the children), materials for making signs, and baskets for displaying produce.

Create a Creature

One way to help children become more aware of the features of different animals is to have them create a creature of their own. In this activity, children use natural materials to design an imaginative creature. As they do so, they draw on what they've observed about the features of familiar animals. They know, for example, that most animals have eyes, a mouth, and a way of moving. They also know that some animals have horns, antennae, or a shell. This activity is designed to foster children's interest in animals and encourage their creativity.

Primary Objective

Children will develop an interest in the physical features of animals by creating a creature using natural materials.

Materials

Modeling clay or playdough
Natural materials, such as leaves, sticks, seed pods, grass, and pinecones
Photos of a variety of animals

What You Can Do

1. Call attention to some pictures of animals, and have the children describe some of the physical features. To focus their attention, you might ask some related questions such as the following:

   - Do you see the ears on the wolf? Do they look like rabbit ears?

   - Look at the feet of the coyote. How are they different from the owl's feet?

   - How does the worm move? Does it have legs?

2. Tell the children that they will be creating a creature of their own. Explain that they can create any kind of creature they want, but it should include some things that real animals have such as ears, legs, antennae, a tail, or wings.

3. Take the children outside and have them collect some natural materials, such as leaves, sticks, seed pods, grass, pinecones, and so on. Tell the children they will be using these materials to create their creatures.

4. Give each child a small amount of modeling clay. Tell them to use the clay to hold the natural materials together as they create their creatures.

5. When they are finished with their creations, have the children introduce their creatures to a friend. In doing so, have them describe some of its physical features and explain how it moves and where it lives.

Additional Suggestions

- Have the children make a habitat for their creature.

- Have the children make toys out of natural materials. Examples of what they might make include boats, dolls, pet rocks, crowns, and drums.

Natural Play Spaces

Schools and city parks often provide playgrounds as a place for outdoor play for children. These playgrounds often feature equipment, such as swings, slides, climbers, and balance beams. Playgrounds dominated by equipment leave children with limited opportunities for engaging in different types of play and seldom invite them to actually experience the ground. The term *playground*, then, isn't a good match to what is actually offered, and many children find such playgrounds boring.

New thinking about connecting children with nature is generating considerable interest in more natural play spaces for children. A natural play space is a space intentionally designed to include natural features for play and active exploration. The intent is to provide enriched play opportunities and to foster understanding and appreciation of the natural world. Some typical features of a natural play space include trees, logs, rocks, sand, varying terrain, pathways, a variety of plants, and places where children can dig or hide. Some natural play spaces also include a garden, some water, and features for attracting wildlife.

Natural play spaces tend to be a lot more interesting and inviting to young children than traditional playgrounds. A natural play space is filled with different colors, scents, textures, and sounds. Children also love the fact that a natural play space is more flexible than a traditional playground. Playground equipment is generally fastened in place and designed to be used in one specific way. Natural play spaces, on the other hand, invite manipulation and change. Children can use their imaginations and creativity to shape the play space in many different ways.

Great outdoor spaces for children respond to what children like to do. While adults may focus on the aesthetics and practical aspects of an environment, children look at an environment and ask, "What can I do?" They want to dig, climb, run, jump, hide, explore, and experiment. They want to pick flowers and splash in water. They want to be independent and have the freedom to initiate activities reflecting their own interests. They want to take risks and make new discoveries. They want a play space they can call their own.

Designing an outdoor environment around the interests and preferences of children can be challenging, especially if we want the environment to accommodate

a wide range of developmental needs and to foster understanding and respect for the natural world. Fortunately, there are guidelines and resources to help us in the process. *Nature Play and Learning Places*, developed collaboratively by the Natural Learning Initiative and the National Wildlife Federation, is an excellent resource for creating and managing places where children can interact with nature. This guide can be accessed free of charge at http://www.nwf.org/what-we-do/kids-and-nature/programs/nature-play-spaces-guide.aspx.

The primary characteristic of a well-designed natural play space for young children is ready access to plants, wildlife, rocks, soil, sand, and so on. Such a play space is highly multisensory, offering rich experiences with sight, sound, texture, temperature, scent, and movement. Materials in a natural play space invite manipulation, construction, and transformation. Many children use the materials to build dens or other types of hiding places. They add leaves and petals to a bucket of water to make soup or tea. They dig ditches and haul rocks. They plant seeds and bury bones.

Natural play spaces can be greatly enhanced by adding a rich variety of loose parts. Loose parts are objects and materials that children can manipulate, change, and move about. While natural materials make excellent loose parts, additional props encourage further exploration and creativity. Funnels and sieves added to a sand box, for example, invite more complex play than just a shovel or cup provide. This added complexity not only enriches children's play, it also extends the time children remain interested in a particular play area. *Loose Parts: Inspiring Play in Young Children* by Lisa Daly and Miriam Beloglovsky is an excellent resource for more ideas on loose parts and how to use them.

Loose Parts to Add as Props

Cardboard boxes, large and small

Large and small pieces of cardboard

Rug samples

Buckets

Sorting trays, such as egg cartons, ice-cube trays, and muffin tins

Cooking utensils

Child-size gardening tools

Baskets of various sizes

Measuring tools, such as measuring cups, rulers, and so on

Clear plastic tubes

Small cars and trucks

Hiking sticks

Small animal replicas

Brushes

Sponges

Wooden planks

Wooden crates

Large pieces of cloth

Drawing and writing materials

Carts

Wheelbarrows

Wagons

Barrels

Old tires

Backpacks

Old cameras

Binoculars

Loose parts are wonderful for their open-endedness. They can be used in many different ways. They can be carried, dumped, dragged, painted, buried, and sorted, and can become almost anything as props in pretend play. Several children using a box with a rope attached demonstrated the open-endedness of loose parts in their natural play space. First, they used the box as a container as they worked to clean up the yard. They filled the box with leaves and sticks that had fallen from the trees as they moved from place to place throughout the yard, dragging the box behind them. When the box was full, they took it to a corner of the yard they had designated as the dump. There they emptied the box and went back for more. They repeated the process several times. The children's next use for the box was hauling sand for a construction project. They soon discovered that sand was a lot heavier than leaves and twigs. They modified their loads accordingly; instead of filling the box to the top, they called it a load after just two buckets of sand. Before the end of the day, the children had decided to paint their box. They wanted to use the box as a sign they could move around announcing a yard sale they were planning.

Play and "Sciencing"

We often think of science as an academic area of study, but it's actually so much more than that—especially in the lives of young children. Science involves observation, exploration, experimentation, and questioning, which is an excellent description of what young children do naturally. We know that young children are curious. We witness this in the questions they ask and in the way they spontaneously explore and experiment. The academic term for this behavior is *scientific inquiry*. Children know it as play.

All kinds of play are motivated by curiosity and questioning. Children want to know what they can do with a stick or what will happen if they spray water on a spiderweb. They'll check to see if a pinecone will float in a bucket of water and will lift a rock to see what's underneath. These activities are forms of scientific inquiry.

Science education in a formal educational setting is sometimes limited to learning facts. This view of science, however, is not consistent with National Science Education Standards and is not the kind of science appropriate for young children. Young children are drawn to "sciencing." They'll poke, pull, lift, push, pound, taste, and shake to see how something works, what's it connected to, and what it's made of.

These behaviors are more reflective of true "sciencing" than the memorization of facts. "Sciencing" suggests active involvement—both hands on and minds on. This means that children should be engaged both physically and mentally in investigating and manipulating elements in their environment. A part of our job is giving them the materials, time, and support for such engagement.

It's appropriate for science education at all levels of education—including early childhood—to address three different areas: content, processes, and attitudes or dispositions. *Content* refers to what we know about the world. Through observation, exploration, and experimentation, children will learn many scientific facts without direct instruction. Their body of knowledge will develop and increase over time. We can support children as they gather information about the world around them by encouraging them to communicate their ideas through words, drawings, and other forms of representation, such as maps, diagrams, and charts.

The *processes*, or *process skills*, represent the active component of science and include such activities as observing, classifying, predicting, hypothesizing, and experimenting. We can support children in practicing and applying these skills by showing a sincere interest in their observations and predictions. We can also provide the materials and settings that invite exploration and experimentation.

Certain *attitudes* or *dispositions*—sometimes referred to as scientific attitudes—are also critical to scientific inquiry. We can support the development of these dispositions by modeling them ourselves and acknowledging them in children. Following is a list of some scientific dispositions.

- Curiosity—The desire to know or learn more about something or someone

- Skepticism—An attitude of doubting or willingness to question what may at first appear true or be stated as true

- Independence—A willingness to figure out something on one's own initiative

- Resilience—The ability to bounce back after frustration or after making a mistake

- Objectivity—The ability to be open minded and free of preconceived ideas. In scientific inquiry, this includes the willingness to discover something different from what you expected. It includes a willingness to withhold judgment.

Ecological Perspective Taking

The ability to think outside one's own world is an important personal, social, and academic skill. It's also critical to the healthy development of one's ecological identity. Thinking outside of one's perspective often takes the form of empathy—identifying with the feelings, thoughts, or attitudes of another. When we speak of ecological perspective taking, we're applying this concept to our relationship with the natural world. Keeping fresh water in a bird bath and walking around instead of through an ant hill can be expressions of ecological perspective taking. Other examples include watering a plant to keep it alive or expressing concern about a bird nest that has fallen from a tree.

You can encourage ecological perspective taking by involving children in caring for plants and animals and by reading books about where and how animals live. You can also encourage children to "become animals" by providing animal puppets and animal costumes.

Water for the Birds

Ecological perspective taking can be fostered in young children by encouraging them to think about what animals need to stay alive. In this activity, children make and maintain a water dish for the birds.

Primary Objective

Children will become more aware of and attentive to the fact that birds need water to survive.

Materials

Bucket
Plastic plant pot with detachable saucer
Water

What You Can Do

1. Ask the children to think of one or two things they need to stay alive. If children don't mention it, tell them that water is one of the things we need to stay alive.

2. Ask, "Can you think of anything else that needs water to stay alive?"

3. After listening to the children's responses, help them understand that all living things need water for survival.

4. Involve the children in setting up a water dish outside for the birds. One easy way to do this is to use a large plastic plant pot with a detachable saucer. Turn the planter upside down, and place the saucer faceup on top of it. Put a stone in the middle of the saucer.

5. For best results, place the water dish near a bush or tree and away from busy places. Birds will feel safer coming to a more protected place.

6. Use a bucket to fill the saucer with water.

7. Involve the children in keeping the saucer clean and filled with water.

Additional Suggestions

- Make a homemade bird feeder with the children, and put it near the birds' water dish.

- In early spring, hang short pieces of string or yarn on bushes and trees to provide nesting material for the birds.

- Read *Home in the Sky* by Jeannie Baker. Talk to the children about birds needing a safe place to live.

Growing Like a Tree

Human connections with trees run deep. We, of course, use trees to meet some of our physical needs. Trees provide food in the form of fruit and nuts. Trees add shade and beauty to our yards, streets, and parks. We use the wood from trees to make a number of products we use every day—paper, furniture, toys, buildings, boats, and fences. We make wooden sculptures and wooden bowls. But our strong connections with trees may also be based, in part, on the fact that trees and humans share similar physical characteristics. We stand upright, have a crown on top, and have mobile limbs stemming from a central trunk. Tubular branches in our lungs have a pattern similar to the root system of many trees.

Primary Objective

Children will develop a deeper appreciation of trees and will become more familiar with the parts of a tree.

What You Can Do

1. Take the children to an outdoor place that has at least two different kinds of trees.

2. Sit or stand by one of the trees. Tell the children to look closely at the tree and share one thing they notice about it. Some responses may be that it's tall, has lots of leaves, has rough bark, has a bird's nest, and so on. Ask, "What should we name this tree?"

3. Sit or stand by another tree. Have the children describe and name this tree.

4. Ask the children to think of one way trees are like people: they're both alive; they both grow; they both need water and air; they both stand up, and so on.

5. Tell the children that the trees they're looking at were once little, just like they were once little. Draw the children's attention to any seedlings that may be growing nearby.

6. Encourage the children to "become trees"—first as little seedlings and then very slowly growing tall with branches stretching up and out. Tell the children to use their arms as branches and their fingers as leaves or needles on the tree. Have the children sway and bend as the wind blows, sag under the weight of snow, and reach their branches toward the sun.

7. Tell the children that there's a part of the tree that they can't see—the roots. Explain how the roots reach down and out under the ground and how the trees use their roots to soak up water. Explain how the water moves up through tubes inside the tree to reach the leaves.

8. Have some of the children stand in a circle holding hands—they are the tree. Have a few other children sit on the ground in the center of the circle. These children are the water. When you say, "Lift," have "the water" stand up, make a slurping sound, and then reach for the branches and leaves of "the tree."

Additional Suggestions

- Give each child a sheet of paper that has been divided into two different sections. Have the children draw a picture of a tree in one section and a picture of a person in the other section.

- Read some children's books about trees such as *The Giving Tree* by Shel Silverstein and *A Tree is Nice* by Janice May Udry.

Dramatic Play

In dramatic play, children pretend to be someone or something else. Imitating what adults or imagined characters do is perhaps the most common form of dramatic play; yet, many children also enjoy being a baby or a dog. With a little encouragement, children will eagerly take on the role of other animals and plants as well. Five-year-old Ryland, for example, recently became a tree.

We had read *A Tree Is Nice* by Janice May Udry and had talked about the many ways trees benefit humans and other living creatures. Ryland climbed up into a tree and was almost completely hidden by the leaves and branches. As I walked by pretending not to know that he was there, Ryland said, "Hey, I'm talking to you." I pretended to be surprised and asked, "Tree, is that you talking to me? Do you have something to tell me?" The tree responded by saying, "I want you to say thank you for all the nice things I do." This conversation continued for some time with Ryland reminding me of the many ways trees enrich our lives.

In this instance, it was the book we read and the conversation we had about trees that inspired Ryland to become a tree. Other props and supports can initiate dramatic play that encourages strong connections between children and nature. Simple costumes, such as a beak, wings, long trunk, or leaves, can encourage children to take on the role of an animal or plant. Of course, becoming a play partner in the pretend situation is probably the most effective way to extend children's dramatic play. Becoming a play partner, however, does not mean taking over or directing the child's play. An adult's participation in pretend play is appropriate when the children take the lead in choosing a theme and determining the direction the play takes.

In addition to supporting children in taking on the roles of animals and plants, we can also strengthen connections between children and nature by encouraging them to take on the role of caretakers of the environment. Start by introducing them to the kind of work done by people directly involved with studying and caring for nature. This could include farmers, gardeners, park rangers, veterinarians, zookeepers, and botanists. You can also introduce children to heroes for the environment through books and stories and then encourage children to "become" these heroes through pretend play. There are a number of books about Johnny Appleseed, for example, that are appropriate for children of different ages. Other children's books about individuals caring for the environment are *The Boy Who Drew Birds: The Story of John James Audubon* by Jacqueline Davies and *The Watcher: Jane Goodall's Life with the Chimps* by Jeanette Winter.

Construction

Construction is a hands-on and sensory-rich type of play. In nature play, children use natural materials to construct places and things. As they do so, they experience and learn about how such materials look, feel, and smell. They also learn how some materials change under certain conditions, such as when they get wet.

Construction can involve making big things, such as dens or forts. It can also involve

making small things, such as corncob dolls or other types of mini creatures. Building dens and forts is an activity that children across cultures have been doing for ages. Children enjoy playing in enclosed places—especially when they have a hand in making them. For some children, the charm of small, enclosed places seems to be the idea that they're out of sight of adults—or at least they think they are. Many children like to make and use enclosed places as props for their dramatic play. They pretend to be animals and need a den in which to hibernate or raise their young. They go camping and construct tents in what they call "wild places." For some children, their enclosed place becomes a clubhouse where only those with the secret code can enter.

Den building doesn't require much in the way of materials. An old sheet and a place to hang it is a good place to start. Cardboard boxes also work great for constructing forts and dens. For natural materials, a good choice is a stack of leafy branches leaning against a tree. If available, dried grasses and leaves make an excellent floor. Most important, however, are space, time, and adult permission. Some adults seem to think that den materials are messy. This may be one reason why den building and other forms of outdoor constructive play are becoming endangered. We may have to change our thinking and our vocabulary when it comes to play materials and play activities for young children.

Constructive play outdoors often involves a wide range of play and social functions. In addition to dens and forts, children—with enough access to building materials—will construct homes, stores, repair shops, vet clinics, and schools. At times, children will create habitats for animals. They may dig an area in the dirt and call it a rabbit's nest. They may spread dried grass under the branches of a bush or between some fallen logs and call it a bed for a baby deer. This habitat building is to be encouraged. It helps children think about what animals need for survival and develops a sense of caring about the well-being of other living things.

A Place to Live

Not all young children will be familiar with the term *habitat,* but they can readily understand the concept behind it. They know that every living thing needs a safe place to live. This activity reinforces this concept while also fostering a sense of caring about other living things.

Primary Objective

Children will gain a deeper understanding of *habitat* and the role a habitat plays in an animal's well-being.

Materials

Lego bricks
Photos of a variety of animals
Photo or replica of a fish
Pipe cleaners
Playdough
Replicas of different animals

What You Can Do

1. Show the children a picture or replica of a fish. Ask, "Can this fish live in a tree? under the ground? in a shoe box?" Listen to the children's replies. Ask, "Where do fish live?" Encourage the children to name some other animals that live in water, such as whales, sharks, and squid, and encourage them to name some other creatures that can't live in water, such as dogs, cats, and butterflies.

2. Explain that the place where an animal usually lives is called a *habitat.* Also explain that for an animal to survive, its habitat must provide safety, food, water, and air.

3. Show pictures of different animals and encourage the children to tell where the animal lives. Also have them talk about how the animal gets its safety, food, water, and air in the place where it lives.

4. Give each child or pair of children a replica of a familiar land animal. One place to get good-quality replicas is Acorn Naturalists (http://www.acornnaturalists.com). Have the children take their animals outside and find or build a habitat for them.

5. Give each child an opportunity to introduce their creature and describe the habitat they made or found and explain how this habitat helps their animal survive.

Additional Suggestions

- Read *The Salamander Room* by Anne Mazer. Have the children draw a picture of a salamander in its natural habitat. Tell the children to include in their picture what the salamander eats, where it gets water, and how it is protected.

- Encourage the children to make a creature using pipe cleaners, Lego bricks, or playdough. Have them build a habitat for their creature using natural materials. Give them time to describe the creature they made and how the habitat meets their needs.

The Adult Role in Nature Play

While a natural play space and access to natural materials are critical to nature play, caring adults also have an important role in guiding and supporting children as they interact with the natural world. Adults should be careful, however, to avoid directing or controlling the play or trying to teach formal lessons during the play activity.

The role of the adult in nature play is to be more of a partner or guide than a teacher or director. The adult's focus should be on fostering a sense of wonder and delight about nature rather than teaching facts. This description of the adult role in nature play may sound sweet and easy, but it is in fact one of the most difficult aspects of our work with young children. Doing it right requires a great deal of observation, insight, and on-the-spot decision making. Without adult support, children's play often falters. It becomes repetitive and lacks intellectual and imaginative challenges. An observant teacher will notice this and provide just the right amount of redirection or support to take a child or group of children to a more satisfying and productive level of play.

Adult play partners understand that young children learn about nature by interacting with it. They learn by constructing their own understandings about the world rather than listening to and accepting what adults may want to teach.

What children need from adults are an inviting environment and the freedom and encouragement to explore that environment. They may need an adult to hold their hand as they walk barefoot through a stream or a listening ear as they make guesses about what they might find if they dig deep down in the dirt.

As responsible adults with young children in our care, we will also be concerned about children's safety. This concern, however, can easily lead to unnecessary constraints on what children are allowed to do. Risk taking is one of the elements that makes play enjoyable and leads to growth in physical, social, emotional, and cognitive areas of learning. Children are generally good judges about assessing a situation and determining what risks they can handle and which ones they can't. They're able to assess their own skills and match them to what the environment or situation might be calling for. Children are also resilient and able to bounce back after mistakes, failures, or even small injuries.

Appropriate risks and actual hazards are two different things. Hazards aren't usually visible to a child. A child may not be aware of a hornets' nest under a deck or the danger of suffocation from a plastic bag. We should be aware of these invisible risks and protect children from them, but it's a mistake to always do the risk assessment for them. Nature play should include some adventurous play. While it's our job to protect children from invisible risks, it's also important to give them rich opportunities to play freely and to have adventures of their own.

Nature play—which often includes discoveries and challenges which children love to share—has a way of fostering positive peer interactions. Teachers can capitalize on this benefit of nature play by supporting and extending what children initiate on their own and with others during their play.

"Hey, look what I found! I think it's a fossil," exclaims a child who just uncovered something interesting as she was digging alone in one corner of the yard. Other children come over to see the "fossil" and then join the first child in an "archeological dig." What began as solitary play by one child soon expanded to become a rich cooperative play experience for a small group of children. The teacher in this case supported the children's play activity by providing additional diggers, sieves, buckets, brushes, and magnifying glasses. She called the children "archeologists" and then explained what archeologists do. She encouraged the children to see how many different kinds of rocks and fossils they could find and to pay attention to where they were found.

Later, back inside the classroom, the teacher encouraged the archaeologists to make a large drawing of the area where they were working and to mark the places where they found the most interesting treasures. This particular group of four- and five-year-olds worked for at least twenty minutes, sharing ideas about what they found and discussing ways to represent their findings in their drawing.

Nature play often includes many opportunities for children to work together to accomplish a common goal. Sometimes, the goal takes the form of construction—as when working together to build a stone-lined path. At other times, the goal might involve negotiating roles for a dramatic play scenario, such as camping, cooking, or having a picnic. Again, the best way for a teacher to support peer interactions during nature play is to provide props as needed and offer ideas only when they add to the richness of the play without taking over the direction of the play.

A challenge for some teachers is to avoid jumping in to solve a problem that surfaces during nature play, such as getting sticks to stay in place as the children build a den or reaching a branch to pick some leaves. Complex cognitive and social engagement often occurs while children work to solve such problems on their own. Teachers would do well to allow this process to unfold on the children's terms and timetable.

While the role should be more of a facilitator than teacher, adults can contribute immensely to the value of what children learn and experience during nature play. Supporting sustained shared thinking is one avenue for fostering learning and attachment to nature. Sustained shared thinking (SST) occurs when two or more individuals work together in an intellectual pursuit focusing on solving a problem or clarifying a concept. SST occurs within the context of a conversation where the individuals involved contribute to the thinking in a serious, extended way. SST with young children can occur between a child (or children) and an adult or between children without the direct involvement of an adult.

When teachers talk to children, it's usually just that—teachers talking with the expectation that children will listen. Teachers tell children what to do or how to do it, provide comments on what children are doing, and give children information. When actual conversations do take place between teachers and children, they tend to be somewhat superficial and short. We sometimes refer to such interactions as "passing conversations." There is a place, of course, for passing conversations, such as in giving greetings or sharing information. But, if our conversations with children are limited to short, superficial exchanges—or focused primarily on giving information—we are missing opportunities to connect on a much deeper and more meaningful level with children's learning and thinking.

Wondering with young children about nature is an excellent opening to SST. It's also an especially effective way of strengthening the connections between young children and nature. Children are naturally drawn to nature and are curious about how it works. Nature, in turn—with all its resplendent beauty and diversity—invites unending questions and offers mysteries to contemplate.

At times, shared sustained thinking will occur naturally between children as they engage in nature play. We can foster such thinking by providing extended periods of uninterrupted time for play in natural environments. New discoveries, rich sensory experiences, and challenges can prompt a level of discussion between children that goes beyond exchanges focusing on routine experiences.

There are times when it's appropriate to join children in nature play and to intentionally introduce and support sustained shared thinking. There are several techniques you can use to do this. One is to ask open-ended questions that invite more than a one-word answer. With open-ended questions, there are no right or wrong answers. Open-ended questions stimulate thinking and the sharing of ideas.

Another technique supporting sustained shared thinking is to make "wondering statements." For example, you might say, "I wonder how a baby bird knows when it's time to peck its way out of the egg." Children are generally willing to share their thoughts about your wondering statements and may then be motivated to make wondering statements of their own.

Narration is another technique supporting sustained shared thinking. Narration, in this context, involves describing what a child is doing. It's not critiquing or praising the work of a child; it's simply describing in words that the child can easily understand. For a child playing with some sticks and sand, for example, you might say, "You're making sticks stand up in the sand." Note that you're not telling the child that it looks like she's making a forest or suggesting that she could make a different arrangement with the sticks. You're just describing exactly what you see the child doing. Typically, a child's response to narration is to provide more information. The child with the sticks and sand, for example, may tell you that she's making a forest, a garden, or a fence. She may then ask you some questions related to what she wants to do. "What else could I put in the forest?" or "Can coyotes jump over fences?" In this way, what started out as a statement on your part might evolve into an extended meaningful conversation where new ideas are developed and shared.

While we want to avoid direct teaching during nature play, we can and should intentionally foster thinking skills in young children. Rather than telling them what to think, we help them learn how to think. We want children to think critically, to question evidence, to formulate original ideas, and to make their own intellectual discoveries. As children investigate and solve problems with each other and with supportive adults, they often develop skills and understandings that they would not develop on their own. We can support such learning by giving children the time to construct understandings and solve problems together rather than simply providing immediate answers or solutions.

Questions to Foster Wonder and Wondering

What do you wonder about?

What do you think?

What would happen if . . . ?

How do you know?

What else do you know about . . . ?

How could we find out?

What could we use?

What else do we need?

What do you think happened here?

Can you tell me more about that?

A part of our role as play partners is to help children develop observation skills. This includes helping children focus attention on different aspects of nature long enough for them to grasp some of the patterns and connections they might otherwise miss. Focusing children's attention can be done in a variety of nondirective ways. We can make suggestions for using different senses to experience and explore the natural world: "I think I hear something rustling in the leaves." "Do you want to feel the smoothness of this rock?" "How many different colors can you see on this leaf?" We can also share some of our own observations: "Something's been eating this leaf." "The ground over here is really hard." "I hear the baby squirrels making a squeaking sound."

Focus Attention

The world of nature stimulates our senses in many ways—through sights, sounds, textures, tastes, and scents. Fascinating shapes surround us, including the shapes we see in constellations and cloud formations. Animals grow in interesting ways and display remarkable behaviors. Plants, too, are fun to watch as they grow and change over time. With so much going on at once, it can be challenging for young children to focus on any specific aspect of nature. We can help them focus attention through playful activities.

Primary Objective

Children will focus attention on the shapes of leaves and will match them to the plants where they grow.

Materials

Paper
Pencils, markers, or crayons
Variety of leaves

What You Can Do

1. Collect different types of leaves from the bushes and trees in the yard. Give each child a leaf.

2. Have the children look closely at their leaves, and encourage them to describe some things they notice, such as color, shape, texture, and size.

3. Have the children find a bush, tree, or other type of plant that has the same kind of leaves as theirs.

4. Invite the children to draw a picture of their leaf and the plant from which it came.

Additional Suggestions

- Focus attention on shapes in nature by giving each child a card with a specific shape, such as a circle, square, triangle, or rectangle, on it. Have them find things in nature that match their shape.

- Tell the children to be very quiet and listen for sounds around them. Have them raise their hands when they hear a sound that is not made by people. Tell them to point in the direction the sound came from and identify what they think is making that sound.

Direct access to nature is more challenging for some children than for others. Children with disabilities, for example, are sometimes left on the sidelines while their peers are actively engaged in nature play outdoors. In fact, some children with special needs find outdoor time to be the most isolating and least engaging time of the day. In addition to a disability, other conditions may interfere with active engagement with nature, such as fear and concerns about getting dirty. As teachers and play partners, we should be keenly aware of what may be keeping individual children from exploring the world of nature and then do what we can to remove or minimize the barriers.

For children with a hearing impairment, stay within their field of vision. This will make it easier to get their attention, if necessary. Use some simple hand signs and gestures to draw attention to what you'd like the children to do.

For children with a visual impairment, provide clear verbal descriptions and many opportunities for hands-on manipulation. You can also add sound features, such as wind chimes, to the outdoor environment to help children with vision problems orient themselves in relation to the source of sound. The sound feature will also add interest to the environment. To maximize the interest and interactivity of the outdoor space, you can also add musical instruments. A marimba or xylophone is great fun, but simpler instruments, such as shakers, rattles, and slap drums, can also be used for making music in the outdoor play space. These instruments, along with many other natural products for an outdoor play space, can be obtained through Nature Explore (http://www.natureexplore.org).

Walking ropes and large push toys are sometimes used for children with little or no remaining vision, to help them move about safely in an environment. Walking ropes consist of one or two ropes running horizontally that the child can use as a guide in moving from one place to another. While walking ropes can help a child feel confident and safe in moving about, they should only be used when really necessary. Large push toys, such as a sturdy toy grocery cart, can also help children with visual impairments move from one place to another. The push toy provides some protection from falls and bumps. Keeping pathways uncluttered is helpful for all children, especially for those with visual impairments or mobility challenges. Another way to help children with mobility challenges, including those in wheel-chairs, is to place a plastic floor runner over grass, sand, and soil.

For a group of children with varying levels of development, provide a wide range of play and learning materials and then allow for a great deal of self-selected activities. For children who are fearful, avoid telling them, "There's nothing to be afraid of," and avoid asking them to touch something they are fearful of. Better to encourage them to watch closely as a creature moves or eats. You might also encourage them to look closely at the creature's eyes, feet, or fur and to describe what they see. When they're ready, fearful children may be ready to feed an animal or put water in its dish. For children who are concerned about getting dirty, make stirring sticks available, place stepping stones across a muddy section of a path, provide a simple washing station outdoors, and use aprons or old shirts as coverups for messy activities.

The early childhood years are important to helping children understand that we should all do our part in caring for Earth as our home. We can show children how to treat the Earth and every living thing with respect. Showing respect includes not littering; not destroying places where animals live; being gentle when handling plants and animals; and conserving resources, such as water, energy, and paper. The best way to teach these respectful ways of caring for the Earth is through modeling. Of course, it's important to be consistent in modeling these behaviors and calling children's attention to what we are doing and why. Instead of telling children what not to do, we can give children positive guidelines for caring for the Earth.

- Trash goes in the trash can. Things that can be recycled go in the recycling bin.

- Know where animals live and respect their homes.

- Be gentle with plants and animals.

- Use only as much as you need.

With a little encouragement, young children will want to be good stewards of the environment. We, as educators, would do well to capitalize on this willingness and give children the guidance they need to relate to the Earth in an environmentally responsible way.

3

Exploration
and Experimentation

. . . .

Exploring Near and Far

When was the last time you thought about what it means to explore and how it feels when you're exploring? Thinking of yourself as an explorer and recalling the excitement you felt while exploring something new will give you some idea of why young children are so drawn to exploring the world around them.

What's in this cave? What's under this rock? What's inside this gourd? These are the kinds of questions that get people exploring. Curiosity and a sense of excitement lead the way. As we explore, we're never sure about what we'll discover. This is what makes it fun.

Young children can be explorers in their own backyards, as there's always something new to discover. One of the interesting things about the natural world is that no two places are exactly alike—each place has its own unique characteristics. The natural world is constantly changing. With a little encouragement, children will want to explore the world of nature and find delight in discovering how it works.

Many young children today spend a considerable amount of time exploring electronic media for the possibilities it has to offer. As a result, they're probably more familiar with the icons on a computer or smartphone than with the plants and wildlife in their own backyards. One way to get children interested in the natural world around them is to help them discover some of the unique features of their immediate outdoor surroundings. Where are the sunny places, the shady places, and the places where you can find worms if you dig in the dirt? Where do spiders like to build their webs? Where do puddles form after it rains? How high in a tree do the birds build their nests? Are there some places where the ground is hard and other places where the ground is soft? You don't have to teach the answers to these questions. In fact, it's best if you don't! Young children will learn more by exploring and discovering than by being taught. Their feelings about a particular place will be shaped by what they can do and discover in that place—not in the facts they learn from others.

Both understandings and feelings play a role in developing a sense of place, which is an important consideration in connecting children with nature. The term "place" in this context means more than a particular geographic location; it refers to the unique character of that place. We can promote a child's sense of place by providing rich opportunities for exploration and manipulation. We can also encourage immersion or immediate encounters with the natural environment. Some practical ideas on how to do this include walking barefoot in sand, grass, or water; playing with water, sand, and mud; burying oneself in a pile of leaves; and crawling under a bush or behind some tall grass.

You can also promote a sense of place by adding some "enchantment factors" to the outdoor environment where children explore and play. These include such things as sunflowers, morning glories, a pumpkin patch, a butterfly garden, windsocks and wind spinners, garden flags, baskets, watering cans, mosaic balls, animal sculptures, and flagstone paths. Such enchantment factors can add to a sense of joy and delight children experience in a particular place. Of course, it's important to use enchantment factors in moderation. The focus should always be on the natural world rather than ornamentation.

A critical factor in making a place attractive and interesting to children is the possibility it affords for active exploration and involvement. We sometimes use the term *affordance* in relation to the play value of an object or place. If our goal is to connect children with nature, we'd do well to consider the affordances that are available to children in the outdoor area where they play. Providing a variety of loose parts increases the play and learning affordances of a place. Natural materials are ideal loose parts; they have different textures, colors, and scents, and they come in different sizes and shapes. Some float, some don't. Some, such as rocks, are heavy; others, such as feathers, are very light. The affordances of loose parts are enormous. They stimulate the imagination, encourage exploration, and invite active manipulation.

Exploring loose parts found naturally in an outdoor area will help children learn the characteristics of that area. Feathers indicate the presence of birds. Leaves on the ground indicate one type of tree, while pinecones indicate a different type of tree. By exploring loose parts found in the natural environment, children will begin to learn the story or characteristics of that particular place. For example, they'll learn from partially eaten leaves that caterpillars, insects, or other creatures have been or are in the area.

Field trips to nature centers and zoos can be educational and exciting, but they aren't necessary for connecting children with nature. Nature can be found right outside the classroom door. Every outdoor space offers access to the sky, air, plants, wildlife, and changes in the weather.

Following are some activities you can use to help children explore the world of nature right outside. Keep in mind, however, the importance of giving children many opportunities to set their own agendas for exploring. Just open the door and let them explore!

Mossy Places

Mosses are flowerless plants. They're usually quite small and grow close together in clumps, often in damp or shady locations. In some places, moss will grow on the lower branches and trunks of trees, giving the appearance of green fur. At times, moss will cover a large area on the ground and may look like a green carpet. Moss can also grow in much smaller patches and appear on walls, rocks, and sidewalks. While moss can grow in almost any part of the country, there is far less moss in the desert than in other places. This is because mosses get their moisture from the air, and the air in a desert tends to be very dry.

Primary Objective

Children will explore the area outside their classroom to look for moss and other interesting plants.

Materials

Moss
Plants

What You Can Do

1. Arrange a display of moss and one or two other kinds of small plants. If you don't have enough moss growing in your yard, you can usually get it from a nursery, as mosses are often used to line hanging baskets and to make terrariums.

2. Ask the children to compare the different kinds of plants in terms of size, color, and texture.

3. Explain that most plants have roots that grow down into the ground but that mosses don't have real roots. Show them the difference. Explain that because mosses don't have roots, they can sometimes grow on rocks and walls.

4. Take the children outdoors and have them search for moss. Tell them to look everywhere—not just on the ground. Each time a child finds moss, encourage the other children to come look at the moss and the place where it was found.

5. After about ten minutes of exploring, give the children a chance to talk about where they found moss. If several children found moss growing on just one side of a tree, rock, or building, you can help them understand why this is so. After this discussion, have the children do a little more exploring to see what other interesting plants they can find. Encourage them to notice where these plants grow.

Additional Suggestions

- Make a terrarium for the classroom. Include moss.

- Display pictures of moss growing on trees and walls.

- Encourage further exploration by giving the children other specific things to look for outside, such as things that are red, round things, smooth things, and so on.

Icy Places

Learning about objects in the sky—sun, moon, planets, and stars—is a part of the science curriculum for children of all ages. Young children learn primarily through hands-on manipulation and exploration. However, the objects in the sky are things they can't manipulate. Instead, young children can learn a lot about the sun by exploring ways in which it affects things on Earth, especially in relation to heat and light. In this activity, children will explore the sun's effect on ice.

Primary Objective

Children will explore the area outside their classroom to look for places where ice melts more slowly than in other places.

Materials

Snow or cubed or crushed ice

What You Can Do

1. Take the children outside on a day when snow and ice have melted in some places but not others. Have the children look for all the places where there is still some snow or ice. Encourage them to look in many different places, even under bushes and around rocks. If you live in a place where snow and ice are rare, simply place some ice cubes or crushed ice in some shady spots and in a few sunny spots. It will melt quickly in the sun, leaving puddles or wet spots.

2. After about ten minutes of exploring, give the children a chance to talk about where they found the snow and ice. If several children found ice or snow on just one side of a tree, rock, or building, you can help them understand why this is so.

Additional Suggestions

- Give each child two ice cubes, and have her place one where she thinks it will melt the slowest and the other where she thinks it will melt the fastest.

- Use a thermometer to measure the temperature in a sunny spot and a shady spot outside.

Let's Find Shapes!

(Activity contributed by Dr. Gwendolyn Johnson)

There are shapes all around us in the natural world! Learning to describe shapes builds children's observation skills and vocabularies.

Primary Objective

Children will describe lines and shapes using words such as *round, curved, straight,* and *bent,* and may begin to use vocabulary such as *rectangle* and *circle.*

Materials

Book about shapes, such as Eric Carle's *My Very First Book of Shapes* or *The Shape of Me and Other Stuff* by Dr. Seuss

What You Can Do

1. Read a book about shapes to the children, such as Eric Carle's *My Very First Book of Shapes* or *The Shape of Me and Other Stuff* by Dr. Seuss.

2. Take the children for a walk outside, and ask them to look for lines that are straight and lines that are curved. For example, they might notice that the edge of a sidewalk is straight and that a tree branch is curved.

3. Ask the children to look for shapes. For example, a brick wall contains rectangles.

Additional Suggestion

If it is not possible to take children for a walk outside, find photographs of the natural world and ask the children to look for straight and curved lines as well as shapes.

The neighborhood around your school can be a great place to go exploring. One of the advantages of exploring the immediate neighborhood is there's no transportation required—you just get out and walk. Yet, there are a few important things to consider when taking children for a walk around the neighborhood.

- Plan the route and destination—check it out by walking it yourself. You need to know that it's safe and accessible. You may also want to identify some interesting things to explore.

- Follow your school's or center's guidelines for taking the children off-site. You may need to get the parents' or guardians' written permission.

- Carry a cell phone and first-aid supplies.

- Take water and snacks, if needed.

- Walk slowly to give the children lots of time to explore along the way.

- Be ready with some ideas on how to keep the children actively engaged. Here are a few suggestions:

  - Give the children something specific to look for, such as a flower with five petals, flying creatures, crawling creatures, or something wet.

- Have the children think of two words to describe something they see.

- Ask them to describe how something feels or smells.

- Have them listen for specific sounds such as a bird, an insect, or the wind.

Some great places to explore while on a neighborhood walk include cracks in the sidewalk, a grassy area at the edge of a parking lot, a nearby stream, and a walking path between some buildings. If you're fortunate, you may also have access to a garden or greenhouse, a park or woods, or a pond or creek.

"What's that?" is a common question many children ask when encountering something new in the natural world. As a teacher, you may find this question a bit intimidating. You may feel that connecting children with nature requires that you know the correct answer. This really isn't the case at all. One of the best ways to connect children with nature is to help them become good observers. Answering "what's that" questions with a one-word answer may actually get in the way of helping children become better observers. Consider the case of a child noticing a land snail on the side of a building and asking, "What's that?" If we tell the child it's a snail,

the conversation—and observation—may end right there. Instead of just telling her that what she sees is a snail, we might say, "Oh, you found a very interesting creature. It looks like it's carrying a shell on its back." With this, the child is likely to look more closely and may even ask a follow-up question, such as, "Is the shell hard?" or "Why is it climbing the wall?"

Perhaps you don't know much about snails at all. That's quite okay. The primary goal for connecting young children with nature isn't about having them learn a bunch of facts about separate pieces of the natural world. Inspiration and enchantment are more important than facts and figures when it comes to connecting young children and nature. Rachel Carson, scientist and author of *The Sense of Wonder*, refers to the naming of things for young children a "game of identification." The value of this game, she says, depends on how you play it. "If it becomes an end in itself, I count it of little use." She asserts that "it is not half so important to know as to feel."

Observation is all about noticing and gathering information about the world we live in. One way to help young children observe more closely is to ask attention-focusing questions. The following examples relate to the child asking, "What's that?" when she saw a snail on the side of a building.

- What do you think the snail is doing?

- How does the snail move—do you see any legs or feet?

- What else do you notice about the snail?

- Do you see anything on the snail that makes it look something like a worm or a turtle?

While these questions will help children notice more details about the snail itself, it's also good to ask questions about how the snail is connected to other things in the environment. After all, nature is a lot more than a collection of separate parts! Connections are essential to the way nature works.

- Where do you think the snail lives?

- If we looked around, do you think we could find other snails living here?

- What do you think the snail eats? How does it get its food?

Again, it's not important to know the answers to these questions. The goal is to foster closer observation, encourage curiosity, and support a sense of wonder. Focusing on habitat is an excellent way to call attention to connections in nature. A habitat is the place that is natural for the life and growth of a living thing. Both plants and animals are living things, and both require habitat for their survival.

Living Things in and around a Tree

Trees are the homes of many animals and help provide the shelter and food they need to survive. Trees also provide habitat for other plants. In this activity, children will look for some plants and animals that live in, on, and around trees and will discover how plants and animals depend on trees in a variety of ways.

Primary Objective

Children will use their observational skills to become more aware of trees as habitats for other living things.

Materials

Tree
Binoculars
Clipboard
Digging tools
Hand lenses
Paper
Pencil

What You Can Do

1. Focus the children's attention on an individual tree. Ask them to be very quiet and to look and listen for any living things that might be using this tree as their home.

2. For each organism they notice, ask them what they think the tree is providing. Is it food, shelter, or shade?

3. After a few minutes, have the children look more closely at the bark and around the base of the tree for other living things or signs of living things. Tell the children that trees can provide a home for other plants as well as animals. For closer observation, provide hand lenses, binoculars, and digging tools. Use a clipboard, paper,

and pencil to record the children's findings. Ask them to look for organisms such as the following:

- Insects
- Worms
- Partially eaten leaves
- Teeth marks on sticks and bark
- Nests or nesting materials
- Feathers
- Fur
- Fungi
- Moss
- Seedlings

4. Ask the children if they know of any other plants and animals that live in trees or use trees for food or shelter. They may be familiar with squirrels, beavers, and ferns.

Additional Suggestions

- Read *A Tree Is Nice* by Janice May Udry.
- Have the children draw a picture of a tree and some of the plants and animals that use the tree for food or shelter.
- Look under fallen branches and decaying leaves for any critters that may be living there.

Life at Different Levels

This activity will focus on animal life at different levels—high in the trees, on bushes, in the grass, and under the ground. Focusing on where animals live will reinforce the concept that, to survive, animals need habitats matched to their needs.

Primary Objective

Through observation and reflection, the children will become more aware of different habitats in which animals live.

Materials

Cutouts or drawings of animals that live in or on trees
Large white cloth
Large piece of poster paper
Marker

What You Can Do

1. Take the children outside and explain that you're going to look for animals that live in different places—some high up in the trees, some on the ground, and some under the ground.

2. Have the children stand near a tree and look up into its branches. Ask questions such as the following:

   - If you climbed this tree way up to the top, what animals might you see living there?

   - If you were on one of the lower branches, what different animal might be living there?

   - Do you know of any animals that might be living on the trunk of the tree or in the bark?

3. Place a large white cloth under the branches of a bush. Gently shake the branches and look for any creatures that fall on to the cloth. These might include spiders, ladybugs, and caterpillars.

4. Ask "What creatures might be living on the ground near the tree or bush or in the grass?" Depending on your climate, the children may suggest grasshoppers, ants, rabbits, or chipmunks.

5. See if you can find any animals or signs of animals, such as tufts of fur, animal tracks, or partially eaten leaves. Look under rocks and other places where creatures might be hiding.

6. Ask, "What creatures might be living under the ground?" These may include worms, moles, and ants.

7. Draw the outlines of a tree and a bush on a large sheet of poster paper. Add cutouts or drawings of animals at the different levels of where they live: high in the tree, in the lower branches, in a bush, and so on.

Additional Suggestions

- Have the children share ideas about how an animal's home can help it survive. They may say that it protects the animal from predators by being high up in a tree or hidden under the ground or that it provides food.

- Have the children share ideas about where they would like to live if they were an animal. Why would they like to live there?

- Show the children a picture of a pond. Have them share ideas about animals that live in and around the pond, such as fish, dragonflies, frogs, ducks, and so on. Have them draw a picture of a pond with wildlife in and around the pond.

As the Wind Blows

While we often see the effects of wind, we don't see the wind itself. This characteristic of wind can make it intriguing to children. Another intriguing aspect of wind is the way it serves as a connector in the natural world. At times, wind carries the seeds of plants and helps birds and butterflies during migration. In this activity, children will focus on the way wind helps plants by spreading seeds to habitats that support their growth.

Primary Objective

Through observation, children will develop an understanding of how wind can help plants by dispersing their seeds.

Materials

Seeds such as dandelion, milkweed, or maple seeds (Use photos if you can't find the real thing.)

What You Can Do

1. Have a small group of children huddle close together on their knees. Tell them to pretend that they are seeds beginning to grow. As they grow, they slowly stand up and reach up and out with their arms. The children will, of course, start bumping into each other. Ask "What could you do to have more room to grow?" Listen to their responses. Explain that seeds don't have legs, so they can't just walk to another place, but that the wind can help them spread out.

2. Show the children some seeds that are often carried by the wind, such as dandelion, milkweed, or maple seeds. If the actual seeds aren't available, use pictures. Talk with the children about how the shape, size, and weight of the seeds help these seeds travel by the wind.

3. Have the children act out the way some seeds are dispersed by wind. Have half of the children huddle close together on their knees. They are the seeds. Have the other half be the wind and blow the seeds across the room or yard.

Additional Suggestions

- Go outside on a windy day. Look for all the things the wind is moving about, such as branches, leaves, seeds, flags, and the hair on each other's heads.

- Fill two medium-sized pots with soil. In one pot, plant several seeds very close together. In the other pot, plant the seeds farther apart. Involve the children in caring for the newly developing plants. After many days, compare the growth of the plants in the two pots. Ask, "Why do seeds grow better in one pot than the other?" Lead the children to the understanding that the seeds are spaced farther apart. The plants have more room to grow. Discuss how both wind and water can help move seeds farther apart.

- Float some seeds in water. Observe how they can float from one place to another.

We use our senses to experience and learn about the world around us. While we usually think in terms of the five senses, as teachers we probably call more attention to sight than any of the other senses. When allowed to explore on their own, however, children are more likely to engage the other senses as well. They'll touch the ice and mud. They'll smell the flowers and listen to the sound of rain on the roof. We could do the same and thus become more interesting partners as we explore the natural world with young children at our side.

In fact, we could also tap into a few more senses now recognized by neuroscientists. These include proprioception, the sense of balance and body position; the somatosensory system, which detects pain, pressure, and temperature; and the vestibular sense, which detects movement and acceleration. We also have intuition, which is sometimes referred to as our sixth sense. Intuition is a way of knowing that doesn't depend on—or goes beyond—reason. It's a kind of inner perception gained through introspection and immediate awareness. Tuning in to intuition sometimes means being more attentive to how nature touches us—not just how we touch it.

As partners in exploring nature with young children, we'd do well to consciously engage all of our senses and encourage children to do the same. Georgia O'Keeffe, a famous American painter of the natural world, encourages us to "touch the flower—lean forward to smell it—maybe touch it with your lips."

One of the major concepts we hope children will gain through their explorations of the natural world is that all things in nature are connected. We want them to realize that what affects one part of nature affects other parts as well. Removing trees from a forest, for example, affects the animals and plants that live in and around the trees. We also want children to become more aware of the general order of many things in nature: Day follows night. Spring follows winter. Seeds sprout into plants. Within this order, there are also variations. An example of this is how plants and animals respond in different ways to changes in the weather.

Hibernation

Many animals hibernate during the winter as a way to conserve energy when food is scarce. As the weather gets colder, they move into a sheltered area and become inactive or dormant. Their body temperatures and heart rates drop. Their breathing slows. Hibernators and deep sleepers eat extra food before they go into their winter homes. It will be several months before they eat again, and the extra food adds fat to their bodies, which helps them stay warmer.

Primary Objective

Children will become more aware of how some animals hibernate as temperatures get colder.

Materials

Crushed ice
Mud
Plastic tub
Replica of a turtle

What You Can Do

1. Ask the children what they would do to stay warm if it got really cold. They may suggest putting a coat on, crawling under a blanket, or going someplace where it's warmer.

2. Ask the children if they have ever thought about what animals do when it gets really cold outside. Some migrate to a warmer place; some grow thicker fur; some crawl into a sheltered place. Explain how some animals hibernate or sleep during the winter— chipmunks go into burrows; toads dig down into the soil; and bears go into caves or dens.

3. Use a replica of a turtle to introduce Tommie the Turtle to the children. (Good-quality replicas are available through Acorn Naturalists at http://www.acornnaturalists.com.) Ask the children if they've ever seen turtles

sitting on logs or on the grass by a pond. Explain how some turtles burrow into the mud at the bottom of the pond and stay there until the weather gets warmer. Demonstrate by burying Tommie in a container of mud. Explain how the mud will help keep Tommie warm even when it snows outside and the water in the pond freezes. Sprinkle some pieces of crushed ice on top of the mud. Tell the children that Tommie will get cold—but not as cold as the ice. Have the children pretend to be turtles and go into and out of hibernation as you describe weather changes from one season to another. You might start by saying it's a warm day and encourage the "turtles" to move slowly from one place to another to look for food. Then describe how the temperature gets colder and the turtles dig in the mud. Explain that the turtles will stay there until the temperature outside gets warmer. Have the children first make their legs stiff, then their arms and upper bodies, and finally their necks and heads. As you talk about the weather getting warmer, have the children gradually "wake up."

Additional Suggestions

- Develop a book about Tommie the Turtle, showing what he does during the different seasons of the year.

- Read children's books about hibernation. Rather than reading straight through these books, call attention to the photos and talk to the children about what each animal does during the winter. A list of recommended books may be found on page 185.

- Have children draw a picture of an animal and show what it does when the temperature gets cold outside.

Animal Homes

All living creatures need shelter and a place to raise their young. The variations in animal homes are tremendous. Some creatures live in water, others on the land. Some creatures live on the bodies of other creatures, and some live under the ground. This activity will help children become better observers of nature by looking for different types of animal homes and noticing the materials animals use to make their homes.

Primary Objective

Children will become more aware of the variety of homes in which animals live and how their homes are connected to the larger environment.

Materials

Clipboard
Pencil
"Where We Looked" chart

What You Can Do

1. Go outside and look for animals or animal homes in a variety of places. For each place, ask, "Why would this be a good place for a creature to live?" Some locations may protect an animal from predators. Some may protect an animal from the hot sun. Some animal homes are located near sources of food or water.

   - Turn over a rock or log. Look for mini creatures living there. Replace the log or rock.

   - Dig in some soil. Can you find any worms or ants?

   - Look in a pile of leaf litter. Can you find any millipedes or pill bugs?

   - Look on the branches, leaves, and flowers of a bush. Can you find any ladybugs, spiders, or caterpillars?

- Look in a grassy area. Can you find any grasshoppers?

- Look up in a tree. Do you see any bird nests?

- Look under the bark of a dead tree or a fallen log. Do you see any critters or tracks made by critters?

2. Record your findings in a simple chart, such as the following.

Where We Looked	What We Found
Under a log or rock	
In the soil	
In leaf litter	
On a bush	
In the grass	
In a tree	
Under the bark of a dead tree	
Other places	

Additional Suggestions

- In early spring, lay out small pieces of yarn and dryer lint for birds to use in building their nests.

- Lay a piece of carpet in a damp, secluded place outdoors. Periodically check for any critters that may have gathered there. Talk with the children about why critters may choose to live there.

- Read some children's books about animals' homes, such as the following:

  Anybody Home? by Aileen Fisher

  Animal Homes by Brian Wildsmith

  Under One Rock: Bugs, Slugs, and Other Ughs by Anthony Fredericks

  A House Is a House for Me by Mary Ann Hoberman

Different Kinds of Rocks

Rocks come in a variety of shapes, sizes, colors, and textures. Some rocks are hard, while others are soft and flaky. This activity helps children focus on the way rocks can differ from each other.

Primary Objective

Through observation and manipulation, children will become more aware of different kinds of rocks.

Materials

Buckets
Digging tools
Everybody Needs a Rock by Byrd Baylor
Paintbrushes
Plastic tubs
Scales
Tempera paint
Variety of rocks
Wagons
Water

What You Can Do

1. Give children multiple opportunities for manipulating a variety of rocks:

   - Washing
   - Stacking
   - Lining a path
   - Weighing
   - Counting
   - Decorating with paint
   - Burying

- Hauling in wagons

- Carrying in buckets

- Rubbing together

- Making a mosaic

2. Read *Everybody Needs a Rock* by Byrd Baylor, and then do the following.

   - Go on a rock hunt for "just the right rock" for each child.

   - Have each child describe one thing she likes about her rock.

   - Have children close their eyes and pick out "their rock" from a pile of rocks.

Additional Suggestions

- Invite a geologist or someone from a rock and gem shop to talk with the children about different kinds of rocks.

- Read *The Rock* by Peter Parnall and *If You Find a Rock* by Peggy Christian.

- Children are more likely to explore if they have some tools for exploring. Here are some ideas:

  - Child-size digging tools

  - Magnifiers

  - Spray bottles

  - Plastic knives

  - Buckets

  - Nets for catching insects

  - Sorting trays

  - Guide books

Experimentation

Experimentation can extend observation and exploration. To experiment basically involves testing an idea. Can I add one more rock to this tower before it falls? What will the ants do if I blow on them? How fast will this ice cube melt if I put it on the hot pavement? In a strictly scientific sense, an experiment must contain a hypothesis and must control for variables. But for young children, an experiment can be a much simpler investigation into something they're curious about. You don't have to be a scientist—or have a strong science background—to guide young children in their experiments. In fact, curious children will engage in a lot of experimenting or investigating on their own, especially if you provide engaging materials, are comfortable with some "messing around," and show an interest in trying out different ideas. An excellent way to model experimentation is to pose the questions that lead to "Let's try it!" responses. Here are some good examples:

- What will happen to water if we pour it on sand, wood, a sponge, hard soil, soft soil, an umbrella, and so on?

- Which will go farther when the wind blows it—this feather or this leaf?

- Will the caterpillar move if I touch it?

- Do seeds always need soil to sprout?

- Will the snail go in its shell if I make a loud noise?

- Will water go through the funnel faster than sand?

In our efforts to connect children with nature, we should always consider the effects our actions will have on the environment. It may be especially important to think about this when conducting experiments. We experiment to see what will happen, and such curiosity should be encouraged. Yet, if we're not careful, our nature-related experiments can have negative effects on the environment and can even influence children to relate to the natural world in less-than-desirable ways. While we work to help children learn, we should also show them how to relate to nature in environmentally appropriate ways. Our goals for children should include the development of respect for and sensitivity toward the world of nature. We want

children to manipulate natural materials, but we don't want them to be destructive as they do so. Here are some basic guidelines to follow in helping children develop environmentally appropriate ways of relating to nature.

- Never strip bark from a living tree or break its branches.

- When collecting plant material, first choose plants and parts of plants that are no longer living. Minimize the amount you take from a living plant.

- If you collect small critters for observation, always treat them with respect. Keep them for only a short period of time, and return them to their natural habitat.

- As much as possible, avoid changing or destroying the habitats of animals.

- Handle all living things—both plants and animals—with care.

- Avoid keeping classroom pets and plants that can't be properly cared for.

Following are a few examples of environmentally appropriate experiments you might conduct with young children. But keep in mind that children should be given lots of support and encouragement in conducting their own experiments.

Seeds in Sand

Most plants depend on nutrients from soil to thrive. The following activity involves children in an investigation to see if plants will grow in sand.

Primary Objective

Children will test an idea by doing a simple experiment.

Materials

Potting containers
Potting soil
Sand
Seeds
Water

What You Can Do

1. Help children notice that most plants grow in soil—even plants growing between cracks in the sidewalk.

2. Ask, "Do you think seeds will grow in sand?" After the children make their guesses, tell them that you're going to try it.

3. Plant some seeds in a pot of soil and the same kind of seeds in a pot of sand. Place both pots in a sunny place. Keep the sand and soil moist.

4. See what happens! Observe the pots over time, and help the children notice any changes.

Additional Suggestions

- Compare what happens when you give two plants—both planted in soil—differing amounts of light or water.

- Expose a plant to freezing temperatures to see what happens.

Worms and Snails

Land snails leave a sticky, slimy trail as they move. Children will see if earthworms do the same. When handling an earthworm, keep its skin moist so it can breathe.

Primary Objective

Children will test an idea by doing a simple experiment.

Materials

Black construction paper
Earthworm
Land snail

Moist paper towel or shallow
dish of water

What You Can Do

1. Place a land snail on a black sheet of construction paper. Wait a bit. Notice the slimy trail left behind when the snail moves.

2. Ask the children if they think an earthworm leaves the same kind of trail when it moves. Try it and see! But keep the worm on a moist paper towel or in a dish of shallow water before placing it on the construction paper. Watch it for a couple of minutes to see if it leaves a slimy trail when it moves.

3. After the experiment, return both the worm and the snail to their natural habitats. Discuss ways in which worms and snails are alike and ways in which they are different.

Additional Suggestions

- Keep one or more land snails in a clear terrarium made of plastic or glass.

- Give the snails two different kinds of food, such as cucumber slices and dandelion leaves. Observe to see which food they prefer.

- Keep one side of the terrarium covered with dark paper or cloth. Do the snails spend more time on the light side or darker side of the terrarium?

Gardening with Children

Gardening with children is an excellent way to connect children with nature and teach them valuable environmental concepts. They learn to care for the needs of other living things. Additionally, gardening fosters motor coordination and the emotional development of young children. As children garden, they experience the satisfaction of caring for something over time and producing something of value. This becomes a source of pride and contributes to positive self-esteem.

One of the environmental concepts children develop as they garden is the understanding of how we depend on the natural world for survival. This understanding, in turn, promotes respect and appreciation for the environment. Gardening with children fosters a sense of wonder and provides many insights into the way nature works. Additionally, gardening activities give children many opportunities to observe, discover, experiment, nurture, and learn. Dorothy Blair, an assistant professor of nutritional sciences at Pennsylvania State University, conducted a review of the literature on the benefits of school gardening and found that gardening promotes children's interest and achievement in science. Gardening also increases their interest in eating a variety of fruits and vegetables.

Gardens can, of course, take a variety of shapes and sizes. While it's ideal to have a section of land in which to garden, wooden boxes and other containers can also be used. Consider planning a garden or section of a garden around a specific theme, such as an alphabet garden, a pizza garden, or Mr. McGregor's garden (from the story of Peter Rabbit). While it's good to grow some fruits and vegetables to help children make the connection between nature and the food we eat, you might also like to plant flowers for the beauty they provide. Some of the flowers might then be shared with others in the community.

An additional benefit of gardening with children is that it can be an effective way of involving them in contributing to the common good. A concern for the common good draws us out of our individual self-interests to thinking about others and how we might help them. Certain types of gardens, such as butterfly gardens and wild-flower gardens, contribute to the common good by providing habitat for wildlife and adding beauty to the community.

Tips for Gardening with Children

- Actively engage the children throughout the process—from planning and planting to tending and harvesting.

- Provide real gardening tools for the children to use. Child-size tools are excellent, but toys are not.

- Set the stage for success. Choose a site with good soil and light, and select plants that are easy to grow in your region of the country.

- Provide a form of boundary around the garden. This might be a low fence, a layer of bricks, or an arrangement of rocks.

- Give children opportunities to showcase their garden. Invite parents and visitors to see what they are doing in the garden. You can also take pictures of the garden and share this through a newsletter, bulletin board, or website.

- Refer to the following resources for additional ideas:

  - Tips for Gardening with Children by Karen Phillips, http://www.naeyc.org/files/tyc/file/Gardening.pdf

  - Gardening with Children, http://eartheasy.com/grow_gardening_children.htm

  - Kids Gardening, http://www.kidsgardening.org

Young children are naturally curious, wanting to know as much as they can about the world around them. In nature they'll find unending opportunities to observe, explore, and experiment. You can support this natural way of learning by going outside with children and becoming their partners and guides in exploring the many wonders of the natural world.

Growing Peas

In most parts of the country, snow peas can be planted outdoors early in the spring. While peas may not be children's favorite food, growing their own often increases their interest in giving them a try. After an initial taste, many young children will actually enjoy the crisp texture and sweet taste of early spring peas.

Primary Objective

Children will gain a deeper appreciation of plants as a source of food.

Materials

Fresh or dried peas*

Planting container or bed

Potting soil

Water

*If you're using dried peas, soak them in water for 24 hours before planting.

What You Can Do

1. Once the danger of frost is over, till the soil where the peas are to be planted. Make finger-size holes in the soil about 1 inch deep and 2 inches apart.

2. Have the children drop a pea in each hole.

3. Cover the peas with soil, and water them. Keep the soil moist by watering almost every day.

4. After a few weeks, look for seedlings to appear.

5. After the plants get a little bigger, blossoms will form and then the peas will appear.

Additional Suggestions

- Make a display of different vegetables with tops, roots, or vines still attached. For example, display carrots and celery with their tops, scallions with the roots and tops, and tomatoes on the vine. Talk to the children about how these foods are grown—above or below the ground, in clusters, and so on. Involve the children in cleaning the vegetables. Prepare a simple dish with some of the vegetables, and make this a part of the children's lunch or snack.

- Read *Stone Soup* (any version), and follow up with role playing the events of the story.

- Visit a farmers' market, and talk to the farmers about how they grow and harvest the food.

4

Indoor/Outdoor Connections

. . . .

Bringing the Outdoors In

It's unfortunate that our society has become so accustomed to thinking of indoors and outdoors as two distinct environments. In many cases, the walls erected between the two become psychological as well as physical. In connecting young children with nature, it would be helpful to minimize these walls and integrate the two environments whenever you can. Spend as much time and energy on developing and using the outdoor environment as we do on the indoor environment. Outdoor time should be an integral part of the play and learning environment.

You can start integrating the two environments by bringing dirt and other natural materials inside and taking books and art materials outside. Consider planting a garden indoors and preparing food outdoors. Use natural materials as manipulatives, decorate the room with natural materials, and display images depicting the natural world. Incorporate nature as a theme for learning centers and group activities. Practice environmental stewardship by recycling and reusing. Invite community members into the classroom to share their nature-related interests.

Take advantage of the light and views of nature that windows provide. In addition to keeping the curtains and blinds open, avoid blocking the windows with objects on the windowsill or furniture in the room. Unobstructed views will encourage children to observe the sky, the weather, and the plants and animals outside the classroom walls.

Many of the natural materials used outside as loose parts can be brought into the classroom as manipulatives. You can bury shells, stones, and sticks in the sand table or use them to extend a playdough activity. Leaves, seeds, and pinecones will float in water or can be used in an art project. Natural materials of all kinds can be sorted, counted, and used as props for dramatic play. Following is a list of ideas for incorporating the outdoors into your classroom activities.

Nature Play Indoors

Focus	Natural Materials	Possible Play Activities
Construction	Twigs, small sticks, sand, soil	Use with toy cars to construct a village on a large tray or box lid
Dramatic play	Seeds, leaves, water	Make "soup" or "tea"
Art	Acorn caps, corn-cobs, pine sprigs	Use with paint to make prints
Math	Seedlings, soil, sand, seeds	Pour sand or soil in sandwich bags and weigh them; sort seeds by size
Science	Twigs, leaves, dried grasses	Build nests in shoe boxes or on shoe-box lids

There are people in every community whose interests are closely connected to the natural environment. You can invite them to share their nature-related activities with the children. It's always a good idea to prepare both the visitor and the children for such visits. Give the visitor some information about your nature-related goals for the children and, if needed, some pointers about how to keep children actively engaged during the visit. You don't want someone delivering a lecture—this just doesn't work with young children!

You can prepare the children by giving them some information about the visitor and his nature-related interests. You can also help the children think of some questions they might like to ask the visitor.

In identifying potential visitors, there's no need to limit yourself to park rangers or naturalists. People who work at public parks are usually wonderful visitors to the classroom and are generally eager to share their knowledge and enthusiasm for the natural world, so you will want to include them. And don't overlook people in other professions:

- Veterinarian
- Zookeeper or educator at a zoo
- Farmer
- Gardener
- Botanist
- Geologist
- Landscaper
- Nature photographer
- Writers and artists who focus on nature

In addition to firsthand experiences with the natural world, children will also benefit from having nature-related books and other informational materials available on a regular basis. Children can learn to use reference books to identify the various creatures, plants, rocks, and weather events they see outdoors. While there are some published guidebooks developed for children, you can also make your own guide specific to your local environment. Of course, it's good to involve the children in making these guidebooks. You can take some photos, and they can draw some pictures. Then, you can put these together in a simple notebook. You can add simple informational text and perhaps some notes about when and where the sightings of each subject occurred.

Cartoon characters and fantasy figures are often used to decorate early childhood classrooms. While children may enjoy them for a short period of time and adults may find them cute, such decorations rarely hold the children's interest over time and have limited educational value. Posters depicting animals in their natural habitat are much more interesting and educational. In addition to using representations of the natural world, you can also decorate the classroom with real natural materials, such as stones, twigs, flowers, leaves, potted plants, and so on. At times, you might also like to set up temporary nature-themed environments in the classroom. You might use a large box in the corner of the room, for example, to create a fox's den or an eagle's nest. In creating a nature-themed environment, involve the children and use as many natural materials as possible.

You may also like to add a variety of animal puppets and animal costumes to the play materials. Encourage the children to pretend to be the animals looking for food and a place to build their nests. Also encourage the children to communicate in the voice of the animal and to move like the animal.

Animals in the Classroom

In addition to having posters depicting animals and their natural habitat, consider making live animals a part of the classroom environment. While one or more pets can be permanent parts of the classroom, other animals, such as insects, spiders, worms, and snails, can be temporary visitors. Collecting animals from their natural habitats for close observation can be a valuable learning experience for young children. In doing so, however, follow some guidelines to protect the safety of the children and the well-being of the animals and to define what children will learn through the experience.

- Choose small animals, such as worms and minnows, rather than ducks and fish.

- Choose only animals that can survive in captivity.

- Choose animals whose habitat can be duplicated indoors.

- Choose a caregiver who is knowledgeable about the needs of the animal.

- Keep the animal for only a short period of time (about a week) and then release it back into its natural habitat.

Plants in the Classroom

Plants, too, can be regular features of the classroom. In addition to different types of potted plants, you can also grow herbs. Cut flowers—while temporary—can add beauty and variety to the classroom while also teaching ecological lessons. Adding wilted flowers to the compost pile will give children the opportunity to learn about decomposition and the life cycle of plants.

Recording and Representing Nature-Related Experiences

One way to extend and deepen children's understandings about the natural world is to help them record or represent what they experience and discover. Their representations might take the form of written narratives, drawings, charts, and graphs. While making charts and graphs is often considered a science and math activity appropriate for older students, these are also forms of communication that even preschool and primary-age children can understand.

Land Snails

Land snails live on land but prefer moist places. They are easy to care for and, in many parts of the country, can be collected from your yard, garden, or woods. Snails are also generally available in pet stores. You can keep several snails in a clear terrarium made of plastic or glass. This will give children an opportunity to watch snails crawl, eat, grow, and breed.

A land snail has a hard shell which provides some protection from predators. The shell also provides a sheltered place to withdraw during dry times. Most land snails move by sliding on a layer of mucus that their bodies produce as needed. In picking them up, it's important to slide them to the edge of the surface rather than peeling them off of it.

Primary Objective

Children will become more aware of how living things have basic survival needs.

Materials

Chalk or crushed eggshells
Clear plastic or glass container
Fruit or vegetables
Land snails
Leaves
Mosquito netting or cardboard
Paper towels
Water

What You Can Do

1. Prepare a land snail habitat in a small terrarium. While almost any clear container will work, you may wish to use a small habitat container, such as those available through Acorn Naturalists or other biological-supply companies. Cover the bottom of the container with several moist paper towels. Add some loose leaves.

2. Talk to the children about what you are doing. Explain that all living things need the right kind of habitat to survive and that a habitat provides food, shelter, air, and water.

3. Place several snails in the terrarium. Add small pieces of fruit and vegetables for the snails to eat. Periodically, add some chalk or crushed egg shells for the calcium snails need to strengthen their shells and help them grow. Mist or spray the sides of the terrarium every few days to keep it moist.

4. Place a cover over the terrarium to keep the snails from escaping. Mosquito netting works well if secured in place. It not only allows the snails to breathe, but it also keeps small insects out. A plastic or cardboard cover can also be used if holes are punched to allow for air circulation.

5. Clean the terrarium at least once a week. Throw away any uneaten food and all accumulated waste. Use wet paper towels or a cloth to clean the bottom and sides of the terrarium. Add clean leaves and fresh food.

6. Wash your hands, and have the children wash their hands after handling a snail or cleaning the terrarium.

7. To place the snails in a type of hibernation called *estivation,* stop providing food and water for days or weeks at a time. This is not harmful to the snails. In a dry environment and without food, the snails will go in to a prolonged state of dormancy.

Additional Suggestions

• Record daily observations of the snails with words and drawings. Record what and how much they eat, where they spend most of their time, and when they seem to be the most active.

• Read *Are You a Snail?* by Judy Allen. Have the children act out parts of the book.

Plants and Plant Parts

Some young children may not think of plants as living things. Their idea of a living thing may be something that moves and eats, and they don't see plants doing either of these. While plants don't have a mouth to eat and drink, they do need food and water to stay alive. For many plants, their roots are critical to getting the nourishment they need to survive.

Primary Objective

Children will understand how roots help plants stay alive.

Materials

Clear plastic cups
Grass seeds
Marker
Poster paper
Potting soil
Water

What You Can Do

1. Plant some grass seeds in clear plastic cups. Start by putting clean potting soil in the cups. Add a few seeds to each cup and moisten the soil. Keep the soil moist until the seeds sprout.

2. Once seedlings sprout, look for roots growing in the soil.

3. Involve the children in doing an experiment with some of the plants. Start by transplanting some of the seedlings from the cups to a larger pot marked "with roots." As you and the children transplant the seedlings, talk about handling the plants very carefully so as not to hurt the roots.

4. As you remove a few other seedlings from the cups, pinch off the roots and transplant them into a larger pot marked "without roots."

5. Keep the soil in both pots moist. Observe what happens to the plants.

6. Involve the children in developing a report about the experiment. Record the steps and observations on a large sheet of poster paper.

   - We planted seeds.

   - The seeds sprouted into seedlings with roots.

   - We planted some seedlings with their roots.

   - We planted some seedlings without their roots.

   - The seedlings without roots died.

   - The seedlings with roots stayed alive.

7. Ask the children to explain why roots are important to most plants. They may say that the roots keep the plant alive, or plants get food and water through their roots.

8. Give each child a sheet of paper with a line dividing it in half. Have them draw a picture of what happened to the seedlings with roots on the top half of the paper and a picture of what happened to the seedlings without roots on the bottom half of the paper.

Additional Suggestion

Do another experiment with seedlings. Use three different pots with the same kind of plants. Give one plant lots of water. Give another plant just enough water to keep the soil moist. Don't give the other plant any water. Watch what happens over time. Develop a report with the children.

Plant Growth

Charting the growth of two different plants is an excellent example of how math and science are interrelated. Basic mathematics concepts addressed in this activity include measuring and comparing, which are called process skills in science. While this activity promotes early childhood math and science goals, it also stimulates an interest in plants as living things and nurtures a child's sense of wonder.

Primary Objective

Children will become better observers of plant growth as they engage in measuring, comparing, and recording the growth of two different plants.

Materials

Flower bulbs in two different sizes, such as paperwhite narcissus
    and amaryllis
Marker
Pebbles or marbles
"Plant Report Form"
Shallow dishes
Water

What You Can Do

1. Show the children bulbs for two different types of flowers, such as paperwhite narcissus and amaryllis. Have the children look carefully at the bulbs and use one or two words to describe how they look.

2. Explain how some plants grow from seeds while others grow from bulbs.

3. Have the children compare the size of the two bulbs and identify which is the larger one. Ask, "Do you think the larger bulb will become a larger plant?" Give children time to offer their ideas. Explain that their guess about which bulb will produce the larger plant is called a hypothesis.

4. Start a plant report by recording the number of children who agree with the hypothesis that the larger bulb will produce the larger plant. Record the number of children who disagree.

5. Place each bulb in a shallow dish. Add pebbles and/or marbles to hold them in place. Keep just enough water in the dish to cover no more than the bottom third of the bulb.

6. Record the growth of each plant on the Plant Report form.

7. After each plant blooms, complete the report by noting what you found out by observing, measuring, and comparing the plants.

| Day | PLANT ONE | | PLANT TWO | | |
	Height	Observations	Height	Observations	What we found out
1					
2					
3					
4					
5					
6					
7					
8					
9					
10					
11					
12					
13					
14					

Connecting through Math

(This section contributed by Dr. Gwendolyn Johnson)

A child picks up small pebbles, one by one, and puts them in a line on the seat of a bench. Another child picks up a leaf that has fallen to the ground and shows it to his teacher. How can we use these opportunities to help children think mathematically?

Mathematics, for young children, is about learning to think quantitatively, in terms of numbers and quantities. This begins very early; for example, children know they have two eyes but only one nose. They know they wear two shoes but only one hat. Our task as teachers of mathematics is to build on this early understanding of quantity by helping children learn to count and develop number sense.

Mathematics is also about learning to consider and talk about the shapes of objects, a skill that will eventually lead to geometry. Young children can begin to think about shapes by describing objects as "flat" or "curved" or "bent" or "pointy" as well

as by beginning to recognize objects that look like squares, rectangles, circles, and triangles. These are skills that go hand-in-hand with learning to carefully observe similarities and differences.

Using nature—or natural materials—can add to the interest of math activities. The richness and diversity of nature stimulates children's motivation. Use objects from the natural world to teach mathematical concepts that are important at the preschool level, such as quantity, shape, and size. Nature is an effective resource for teaching and learning mathematical concepts.

Let's Sort!

Sorting and classifying, such as classifying numbers as either even or odd, is common in mathematics. Putting objects into groups encourages children to think about similarities and differences among the objects.

Primary Objective

Children will develop sorting skills by placing objects into groups.

Materials

10–20 objects in one category, such as flowers, rocks, or leaves
Book about sorting, such as *Sorting* by Henry Arthur Pluckrose
  or *Sorting at the Market* by Tracey Steffora

What You Can Do

1. Read to children a book about sorting, such as *Sorting* by Henry Arthur Pluckrose or *Sorting at the Market* by Tracey Steffora.

2. Provide children with ten to twenty objects from the natural world that can be sorted, such as leaves of different colors or shapes, flowers of different types or colors, pebbles and rocks of different sizes, and so on.

3. Ask the children to notice differences among the objects. Children might mention the size, shape, color, or texture of the objects. Accept all answers, but encourage children to focus on an attribute that will make it easier to sort the objects.

4. Help the children sort the objects into two or three piles. Encourage them to talk about how they are sorting the objects by asking questions such as, "What can you tell me about the objects in this pile?"

Additional Suggestion

Help children notice that objects can be placed into various categories such as "things that are blue" and "things that are flat." This can be done by playing an I Spy game. Say, for example, "I spy something blue." Then, encourage the children to notice blue objects. By noticing similarities among objects, children can sort and categorize items without physically moving the objects into piles or groups.

Which Is More?

Children can identify which of two groups contains more items even before they have learned to count. A desire to identify which is more helps children see the usefulness of counting.

Primary Objective

Children will extend their understanding of *more* by comparing quantities using counting or other methods.

Materials

10–20 objects in one category, such as flowers, rocks, or leaves
Book about *more* and *less,* such as Tana Hoban's *More, Fewer, Less*

What You Can Do

1. Use a book with photographs to help children consider the ideas of *more* and *less,* such as Tana Hoban's *More, Fewer, Less.*

2. Using the objects you sorted in the Let's Sort! activity, ask the children to notice which group has more and which has less.

3. Without removing or adding any items, rearrange the objects so that each group is arranged in a line rather than a pile. Again, ask "Which group has more?" and "Which group has less?" Rearranging objects helps children achieve the notion of conservation, the idea that the arrangement of the objects does not affect the quantity. For example, ten acorns in a line is the same amount as ten acorns in a pile.

Additional Suggestion

Begin asking about *more* and *less* with small groups of objects, perhaps fewer than five objects in each group. Children will be able to determine which group has more without counting. Gradually increase the number of objects in each group. Once each group has more than ten objects, children will likely need to count to determine which group has more.

Exploring *More*

More in mathematics refers to a greater number, as in, "Nine is more than five." However, *more* in our everyday usage can refer to the size of an individual object; for example, a large piece of cake is more than a small piece. This activity will help children begin to understand *more* in the mathematical sense.

Primary Objective

Children will use counting skills to further develop their understanding of the concept of *more,* beyond simply "which one is bigger."

Materials

Objects of different sizes, such as rocks and pebbles

What You Can Do

1. Once children are comfortable with counting and comparing groups based on the number of objects, ask them to compare one large object, such as a large rock, to a collection of smaller objects, such as a collection of pebbles or acorns. Many young children will say that the large object is "more" because it is larger.

2. Ask children to count the number of objects in each group.

3. Again, ask which group has more. Help children reach a conclusion such as, "This group with a rock has one, and this group of pebbles has seven. There are more pebbles than rocks." This activity will help them push beyond their prior understanding of *more*—that the bigger object is "more." Relying on counting rather than their eyes takes some logical, abstract thought.

Additional Suggestion

Create a collection of objects and ask children to create a group with more, the same, or fewer. For example, you could say "I have six green leaves. Can you show me a group that has fewer than six leaves?"

Which Is Longer?

Measuring is an important part of mathematics at all levels. Helping children understand the concept of measurement in preschool can prepare them for more complex measurement concepts and activities in elementary school. Comparing objects by placing them next to each other is called *direct comparison.* This type of measurement does not require any units such as inches or centimeters.

Primary Objective

Children will be introduced to the vocabulary *longer than* and *shorter than.*

Materials

Variety of objects of different lengths

What You Can Do

1. Obtain several natural objects of various lengths. Try to obtain objects that are longer than they are wide. This will help children focus on the length rather than on the overall size of the objects.

2. Discuss with the children what the objects are and where they were found.

3. Ask the children to make observations about the objects. For example, they may say that a twig is rough or that a feather is soft or smooth.

4. Place two objects next to each other, and ask the children which object they think is longer. Show the children how to align the tips of the objects so that the lengths can be accurately compared.

5. When the children seem to understand *longer than* and *shorter than* with two objects, repeat with three or more objects.

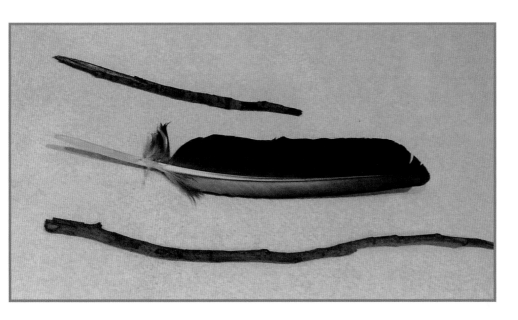

Additional Suggestions

- The length of curved objects can be measured by laying a piece of yarn alongside the object and then cutting the yarn to match the length of the object. Compare the lengths of curved objects by comparing the lengths of the pieces of yarn used to measure them. Children enjoy estimating which of two curved objects is longer and then measuring to determine if their prediction was correct.

- Provide children with some photographs of snakes that are coiled and other snakes that are not coiled. Discuss with the children the lengths of the snakes. Young children may not realize that the length of an object does not change when it is coiled or uncoiled. Demonstrate coiling a piece of yarn to show children that the length remains the same. Ask children to draw pictures of snakes and discuss their lengths.

Which Is Bigger?

Measuring with everyday objects such as pennies is called *informal measurement.*

Primary Objective

Children will be introduced to informal measurement as they compare the sizes of leaves.

Materials

Flat leaves in a variety of sizes
Pennies

What You Can Do

1. Provide children with two or more flat leaves, or ask them to collect leaves from outdoors.

2. Discuss the leaves with the children, asking them about the leaves' colors, shapes, and sizes, and where the leaves were found.

3. Ask the children to compare the sizes of two or more leaves by asking, "Which one do you think is bigger?" Use vocabulary such as *longer, shorter,* and *wider.*

4. Tell children that we can find out which leaf is bigger by covering the leaves with pennies. Help the children cover each leaf.

5. Help the children count the pennies on each leaf to determine which is bigger.

Additional Suggestions

- A wide variety of objects such as paper clips and cereal can be used as measurement tools as children explore informal measurement. Let the children explore measuring with several types of objects.

- Read a children's book about size such as *Big and Small* by Britta Teckentrup or *Is it Big or Small?* by Bobbie Kalman.

Is It Half?

Fractions are notoriously difficult to understand for both children and adults! You can help young children begin to understand *half* by pointing out things that are separated approximately into halves. Children who have a sibling may have already been introduced to the idea of *half,* if they are expected to share food or other items with their sibling.

Primary Objective

Children will be introduced to or become more familiar with the words *part* and *half* and will begin to understand estimation words such as *about.*

Materials

Crayons
Paper
Variegated leaf or rock

What You Can Do

1. Look for objects from nature that contain different textures or colors within one object, such as a leaf with more than one color or a rock with more than one texture.

2. Discuss the objects with the children, using the word *part* as appropriate, such as, "The leaf is part green and part red." If one of the objects is approximately half of one color and half of another, introduce the word *half* and explain that it means that the two sections are about the same size.

3. Ask the children to draw a flower, tree, leaf, rock, or similar object and make part of the object one color and part of the object another color, or ask them to make half of the object one color and half another color.

Additional Suggestion

Read children's books that feature the word *half,* such as Shel Silverstein's *A Giraffe and a Half.* Discuss with the children what *half* means in relation to the book.

Nature provides a complex and stimulating environment in which to extend children's thinking about numbers and shapes. You can support children's mathematical development by helping them learn to count objects around them, sort objects based on similarities and differences, and describe shapes using both informal language and the language of geometry.

5

Connecting through Language,
Literacy, and the Arts

• •

Stories and Poems

Sharing stories and poems with children is an excellent way to help them develop language and early literacy skills. Stories and poems can also be used to promote understandings and positive attitudes about the natural world. Many young children have heard stories about the "big bad wolf" and may think of wolves as mean and dangerous. Fortunately, there are books offering more positive and accurate views of wolves and other parts of nature that have been misrepresented in children's literature. Books with positive messages about the natural world are sometimes referred to as *pronature books*.

A pronature book will usually meet one or more of the following criteria:

- Gives a message about nature being more than something to be used by people—that it's also a source of wonder and something to be respected

- Provides an accurate portrayal of nature and the way it works

- Includes suggestions about how to relate to the natural world in a caring way

You might find the following resources helpful in finding children's books with pronature messages.

In addition to both fiction and nonfiction books, nature-focused poetry can also be used to help connect children with nature. A nature-focused poem includes some

aspect of nature as its theme and often invites philosophical reflection on the wonders of the natural world. "Who Has Seen the Wind?" by Christina Rossetti is an example of a nature-focused poem.

> Who has seen the wind?
> Neither I nor you.
> But when the leaves hang trembling,
> The wind is passing through.
> Who has seen the wind?
> Neither you nor I.
> But when the trees bow down their heads,
> The wind is passing by.

Some of the benefits children are likely to gain from this poem include a deeper understanding and appreciation of wind, an inclination to become more observant of natural phenomenon, an appreciation of poetic expression, and the development of language and early literacy skills.

The world of nature offers incredibly rich sensory experiences—from the warmth of sun on our skin to the sweet taste of freshly picked strawberries. Poetry tends to be more effective than other forms of language in capturing the essence of these experiences. Poetry also has an almost magical way of introducing new ideas or ways of seeing things. The poem "Who Has Seen the Wind?" for example, introduces the idea of leaves trembling and trees bowing their heads. While these images of leaves and trees may be new to young children, they readily move beyond the literal and imagine things in nature sharing human feelings and behaviors. We often see this in nature play as young children take on the roles of animals or other aspects of the natural world.

Picture books are sometimes written as poems and can be used to foster poetic thinking in young children. Some nature-focused picture books with poetic text include *I Love Our Earth* by Bill Martin Jr. and Michael Sampson, and *Flower Garden* by Eve Bunting. Other picture books, while not written as poems, still present poetic images. Several favorites with clear environmental themes include *The Other Way to Listen* by Byrd Baylor and *All the Colors of the Earth* by Sheila Hamanaka.

Playing with the Wind

We often say that young children learn by doing—that they need to manipulate materials to construct their own understandings about the world around them. But physical manipulation isn't enough. Children need both hands-on and minds-on manipulation. This is especially true in learning about the natural world and how it works. Children can experience or observe such phenomena as gravity, buoyancy, and the wind, for example, but their ability to physically manipulate them is very limited. To really appreciate and understand such phenomena, children will need to become mentally engaged with the concepts. We can help them do this through guided activities paired with philosophical discussions.

The poem "Who Has Seen the Wind?" can be used as an introduction to a philosophical discussion with young children. Most children are familiar with wind as something that can cause branches to move and flags to wave. A related concept they may never have considered is the fact that they can't really see the wind—they can only see its effects. Engaging children in a philosophical discussion about this concept will help them mentally manipulate related ideas and, in the process, construct their own understandings about the world.

Primary Objective

Children will participate in a philosophical discussion about things that are real but can't be seen.

Materials

Copy of the poem "Who Has Seen the Wind?" by Christina Rossetti
Windy day

What You Can Do

1. Take the children outdoors on a windy day. Have them look around and list some of the things they see, such as trees, cars, grass, clouds, leaves, and so on.

2. Encourage further discussion by asking the children to describe what they notice about some of the things they listed. Focus on things that are moved by the wind. "What do you notice about the trees? about the branches? about the leaves?"

3. Continue the discussion by asking questions about what it would feel like to be the leaves or the trees.

4. Invite the children to move like leaves or branches on a windy day. Encourage them to use their arms and legs, their hands and feet, and their entire bodies to show what it's like to be blown about by the wind.

5. Have the children sit or lie down on the ground with their eyes closed. Tell them to think about the wind. After a few minutes, invite the children to share their ideas about the wind and how it feels.

6. Share the poem, "Who Has Seen the Wind?" by Christina Rossetti. Read or recite the poem a second time and then ask, "Who has seen the wind?" By now, some children may be ready to say, "not me and not you." If not, read the poem again and note what it says about not being able to see the wind.

7. Ask, "If we can't see the wind, how do we know it's there?"

8. Ask for other examples of things that are real but can't be seen, such as the chime of a bell, the air in a balloon, or the way we feel when we're hungry.

Place-Based Education

Connecting children with nature is more about nature in their own backyard and community than nature in faraway places. We want children to know nature as something that is real and relevant to their personal lives. Place-based education (PBE) emphasizes the idea of having children engaged with the actual environment they are learning about. PBE also focuses on the idea of a sense of place. *Place*, when used in this context, means more than a geographic location; it includes opportunities for seclusion, for exploring, for changing things about, for immediate encounters with the natural world, and for memorable moments. Natural play spaces for children are designed to offer such opportunities and are ideal for promoting the goals of place-based education.

Scavenger Hunt

A well-planned scavenger hunt can engage children in closely observing the local environment. Talking to the children in advance can help them understand how environments can differ from one place to another.

Primary Objective

Children will develop a sense of place about their local environment.

Materials

Index cards
Marker
Star stickers

What You Can Do

1. For advance preparation, identify eight different natural items outdoors that the children can look for during a scavenger hunt, such as the following.

   - Leaf with three points
   - Tree with moss on its trunk
   - Animal footprint
   - Feather
   - Spiderweb
   - Seed pod
   - Wet grass
   - Partially eaten leaf
   - Ant

2. Tell the children that they will be going on a scavenger hunt. Explain that a scavenger hunt is a kind of game where they search for specific things on a list. Tell them that everything on their scav-

enger list is something natural that can be found outside. Explain the difference between things that are natural and things that aren't natural.

3. Put the children in groups of three or four. Give each group the name of a native animal, such as an eagle, an owl, a fox, or a coyote. Have one child in the group hold a card with their group's animal name.

4. Go outside with the children. Explain any necessary rules about where they may go while searching.

5. Tell the children that there are eight different things on the scavenger list, but that they will look for just one thing at a time. Tell them that you will call out the name of what to look for and that they should raise their hands when they find it. Put a star on the back of the group's card each time their group finds an item.

Additional Suggestions

- Play an I Spy game focusing on natural items in the yard.

- Have the children participate in making an alphabet book or alphabet chart with the name of natural items found in the local environment. You might make this a project that extends over a period of several days or weeks to give the children plenty of time to add their suggestions. They may even wish to ask their families for suggestions.

- Read some children's books about nature in one's own backyard, such as *In My Backyard* by Valarie Giogas and *In My Backyard* by Margariet Ruurs.

Use place-based stories to promote positive connections with the local environment. A place-based story uses local settings and local characters. There aren't many published books for children focusing specifically on the environment where they live. Some creative teachers are developing their own place-based stories and, at times, involving the children in the process.

You can do this, too. Start with choosing an animal that lives in your area. Develop a story with that animal as the main character or as an important character in the story. The story can be very imaginative, with the character taking on a fantasy role, or more informative, with factual details about the animal and its habitat. A fantasy story might be a legend or folk tale, giving an explanation about how something in nature came to be. There are Native American legends, for example, about how turtle got its shell and how summer and winter came to be. A more informative story, on the other hand, would be more like some of Eric Carle's books, such as *The Grouchy Lady Bug* and *The Very Hungry Caterpillar*.

Another way to develop place-based stories is to focus on special places in the local natural environment. You might start by sharing memories of a special place you had as a child, such as a "secret place" in a woods, a stream or pond where you went fishing, or a tree house where you often played. You can talk to the children about why you liked this place and what it made it special.

In sharing your place-based story, you'll want to do more than just tell the story. You'll want to make it animated and to involve the children. Avoid sitting still in a chair. Vary the rhythm of your speech, and use body language and props. Walk around and find ways for the children to participate. They may act out parts of the story as you tell it. They might repeat dialogue, contribute sound effects, and answer questions.

After sharing your story, you can then encourage the children to describe their special places. Use some guiding questions to help them through the process:

- What does your special place look like?

- What does it sound like?

- What do you like to do in your special place?

- What makes it special?

You might also provide them with props for telling their stories. You can have the children draw pictures of their special places highlighting the features that are most important to them.

Another idea for developing place-based stories starts with a walk to a natural area in the community. This area might be a park, a stream, or a wooded area. Spend some time thinking about the natural features of this area. You may wish to take notes as the children share their observations. If the children are old enough, they may also take notes or draw pictures. Again, guiding questions may help them through this process:

- What animals live here?

- How are their needs met?

- What do they eat?

- How are they protected?

- What kinds of plants grow here?

- Are there any trees?

- How big are they?

- Are they growing close to each other?

- Are there any seedlings?

- Have any of the trees died?

- Is this a sunny place or a shady place?

- Where does the water go when it rains?

- Does it sink in to the ground or run off to someplace else?

- Is the ground in this area hard or soft?

- Is the ground sandy or more like clay?

- How are natural things in this area connected?

Back in the classroom, you may have the children draw a picture of the natural area. If they're old enough, you may have the children draw a map of the area indicating the location of some of the major features of the place. You might also have the children make a large mural of the natural area highlighting the features they liked the most.

Nature Journals

One way to generate interest in nature and to increase observational skills is to have children keep nature notebooks or nature journals. A nature journal is a recording of what is seen or experienced in nature. Keeping a nature journal can

help children slow down and really focus on the world around them. As they record their observations and feelings, children will become more aware of what nature is and what it means to them.

Connecting through Music

Music has an almost magical way of inspiring young children to learn about and care for the natural world. There are a number of ways to use music to strengthen the connections between children and nature. You might start by helping children listen to musical sounds made by birds, insects, wind, and rain. Then ask them to draw pictures of what made the sounds they heard.

Another way to use music to strengthen children's connection with nature is to make musical instruments using natural materials. A container with a lid, such as a coffee can, a plastic jug, or a cardboard cylinder, and some seeds are all you need to make a shaker. Each type of container will make a unique sound. If the container doesn't come with a lid, you can make one by taping a piece of cardboard or other sturdy material over the top. Use the shaker as a percussion instrument as you sing or play some music.

Stories about Where We Live

Some children's books are about faraway places and exotic animals. While these books can be helpful in fostering awareness of a larger world, place-based stories help children become more interested in their own local environment.

Primary Objective

Children will develop an increased interest in their natural local environment through stories about an animal that lives in that environment.

Materials

Photo of a local animal species
Props (These will vary by story.)

What You Can Do

1. Choose an animal native to the local environment. Obtain a picture of that animal and some basic information about it—for example, where it makes a nest, what it eats, and how it moves.

2. Develop a fictional story about that animal, and gather some props for telling the story, such as nesting materials or a picture of something the animal eats.

3. Introduce the animal, and then tell the story using the props.

4. Invite comments about the animal and some of the things it does in the story. Also invite children to extend the story by suggesting other things the animal might do.

Additional Suggestions

- Have the children draw pictures for the story you shared. Then use their pictures to illustrate the story in a book format.

- Encourage the children to choose a native animal and have them develop a story around that animal. Give them time to collect some props and then share their stories.

Make a Nature Notebook

Nature notebooks are easy to make. Involving children in making and decorating their own nature notebooks will increase their interest in using them.

Primary Objective

Children will develop an increased interest in the natural world by making and using their own nature notebooks.

Materials

Card stock, thin cardboard, or manila folders
Hole punch
Markers or crayons
Paper
Twist ties

What You Can Do

1. Give each child five to ten sheets of paper with prepunched holes for binding. Also give each of them two sheets of card stock, thin cardboard, or a manila folder cut in half along the fold, also prepunched. The pieces of card stock or cardboard should be slightly larger than the paper.

2. Show the children how to put their notebooks together by using the sheets of card stock or cardboard as the front and back covers. Help them use twist ties to hold the notebook together.

3. Have the children draw a picture of one of their favorite things in nature on the front covers of their notebooks. Also have them write their name on the cover.

4. Have the children take their notebooks outdoors and find a special spot to observe nature. As they sit quietly in their special spot, have them draw a picture and/or write about what they observe and how

they feel. Tell them to use just one or two pages of their notebook so that they can use the other pages on different days.

5. Take the children outdoors to revisit their same special place a number of times. With each visit, have them add one or two more pages of drawings and notes to their notebooks.

Additional Suggestions

- Work with the children to keep a log of the number and types of birds that come to a birdfeeder in the yard.

- Work with the children to keep a log of how their plants grow after they plant some seeds or seedlings.

Sounds of Music

Calling attention to musical sounds made by nature is one way to foster sensitivity to nature. Most children are familiar with the idea of birds singing, but they may not have considered other sources of musical sounds heard in the natural world. If they listen, they can hear insects buzz, brooks babble, leaves rustle, and rain patter. Musical sounds in nature—in addition to providing a pleasant aesthetic experience for young children—can also evoke positive emotions.

Primary Objective

Children will become more aware of musical sounds heard in nature.

Materials

Recording of "The Sound of Music" from *The Sound of Music* by Rodgers and Hammerstein

What You Can Do

1. Have the children close their eyes and think about walking through a hilly place on a nice sunny day. Ask, "What do you think you might see as you walk through these hills?" "What would you hear?" "How would you feel?"

2. Tell the children that someone once wrote a song about musical sounds they heard in nature. Explain that the title of this song is "The Sound of Music." Tell the children to listen very closely as you read words from the song. Tell them that as they listen, they should make pictures in their minds of what the words say.

3. Read two or more verses of the song. Invite the children to share their favorite parts of the song and then draw a picture of it.

JOIN US
DECEMBER 21-24

---

10 CHRISTMAS SERVICES

THURSDAY - 8:00 PM

FRIDAY - 8:00 PM

SATURDAY - 5:00 PM | 6:30 PM

SUNDAY - 8:15 AM | 9:45 AM | 11:15 AM
12:45 PM | 5:00 PM | 6:30 PM

THEFELLOWSHIPCHURCH.COM
4873 LONE TREE WAY, ANTIOCH, CA 94531
(925) 755-3040

HOPE FOR TOMORROW • HEALING FROM YESTERDAY

Christmas Eve

Candlelight Experiences

Fellowship Church

Additional Suggestions

- Have the children watch the film *The Sound of Music* during the part when the song "The Sound of Music" is sung.

- Listen to nature-inspired music, such as *The Four Seasons* by Antonio Vivaldi and *Water Music* by George Frideric Handel. Invite the children to share their thoughts and feelings about this music. Also have them draw pictures of what they see in their minds as they listen to this music.

- Share recordings of nature sounds. Free downloads are available at http://www.naturesongs.com. Have the children imitate some of the nature sounds.

- Share children's books about listening to nature, such as *The Listening Walk* by Paul Showers and *The Other Way to Listen* by Byrd Baylor.

Invent an Instrument

A variety of musical instruments, such as drums and clappers or clapsticks, can be made using sticks and stones. With a little encouragement, children will find a number of ways to make their own musical instruments using natural materials. This is a good way to help children focus on some of the unique characteristics of materials found in nature.

Primary Objective

Children will become more familiar with the characteristics of natural materials by using them to make musical instruments.

Materials

Variety of natural materials, such as sticks, grass, and rocks

What You Can Do

1. Ask the children to think of ways sticks, grass, rocks, or other natural materials might be used to make musical instruments. After sharing some ideas, ask the children to experiment with different natural materials to make their own instruments.

2. Play or sing some music with the children accompanying on their instruments.

Additional Suggestions

- Demonstrate how a blade of grass held between your thumbs can be used as a whistle.

- Demonstrate how striking a hollow log with a stick makes a different sound than striking a log that isn't hollow.

- Show the children some pictures of the Cochiti Pueblo drums (available on the Internet). Explain some background about the Cochiti people and how they use natural materials to make drums. For more information, see http://www.pueblodecochiti.org.

- Show the children some pictures of a ram's horn, called a shofar (available on the Internet). Explain how it is sometimes used as a trumpet.

- Songs with environmental messages can strengthen children's connection with nature. You may wish to check out the following for some nature-related songs:

  - Schnetzler, Pattie. 2003. *Earth Day Birthday.* Nevada City, CA: Dawn.

  - Weeks, Sarah. 1994. *Crocodile Smile: 10 Songs of the Earth as the Animals See it.* New York: Scholastic.

  - The Acorn Naturalist website includes a list of children's songs about nature. Visit http://www.acornnaturalists.com/store/Science-and-Nature-Music-for-Young-Children-C833.aspx.

Movement

Play in natural environments includes a great deal of movement. Children dig in the dirt and sand, carry stones and pails of water, drag large branches, climb over logs, roll down hills, and reach to pick leaves from overhead branches. While they need little encouragement to be active outdoors, some suggestions and guidance can strengthen their connections with nature as they move about outside. You can start by calling attention to the movement of things in nature, and then encourage children to imitate those movements. You might, for example, spend time with the children observing birds as they soar in the sky, water as it flows over rocks in a stream, or butterflies as they dance from flower to flower. Then, suggest that the children engage in a dance of their own, imitating movements they observe in nature.

You can also encourage children to act out other phenomena they see in nature—a seedling growing into a tall tree, a butterfly emerging from a chrysalis, or a bird hatching from an egg. They can become leaves on a tree blown by the wind, a rabbit hopping across the yard, raindrops bouncing off of an umbrella, or clouds moving across the sky.

Drawing, Painting, and Sculpting

Encouraging children to draw, paint, and sculpt elements of nature is an effective way to focus their attention on the beauty and wonders of the natural world. While traditional materials can be used in creating works of art, nature itself offers many items that can be used as art tools. Pine sprigs and stalks of wheat can be paintbrushes. Berries and dandelion blossoms can be used instead of crayons. Corncobs can be used instead of rolling pins to roll out clay.

You can also incorporate natural materials into works of art. Use leaves, seeds, and flower petals in collages. Use corn silk and milkweed fluff as hair when creating three-dimensional figures. Use cattail leaves and ivy for weaving. Use a stick to draw designs in mud or sand.

Children's earliest drawings are typically just lines on paper, as children at this stage are exploring how different materials work. As children get a little older, they begin to draw in a more purposeful way. They try to represent objects, people, and events.

One way to connect children with nature at this stage is to help them see and draw some of the small stuff in nature. As children draw a tree or cat, for example, you might encourage them to add the design in the bark of the tree or the whiskers on the cat.

As children get the idea of drawing what they see, they'll probably start noticing and drawing more details in the world around them. They may, for example, draw the veins of a leaf or a ladybug on a log.

Drama

We often use the term *dramatic play* interchangeably with *pretend play*. For some, this might suggest that drama and pretend play are the same thing, but there are some differences. Drama is more of a performance based on a preset story; while in pretend play, the story evolves as children pretend to be someone or something different from themselves. Both drama and pretend play have benefits for children, and both can be used to deepen children's connections with nature.

One way to connect children with nature through drama is to have them act out a story from a pronature book or an idea from a nature-related poem. The children might take on the role of almost anything in the story or poem—a person, an animal, a plant, and so on. Costumes and other types of props will help them play their parts. In a dramatic performance of *Once There Was a Tree* by Natalia Romanova, for example, children can pretend to be the old tree, the woodsman who cut it down, or one of the animals—the titmouse, earwig, ants, bear, frog, and beetle. Individual children can also take on the roles of the sun, clouds, rain, thunder, or lightning. With younger children, you can narrate the story while the children act it out. With older children, you may have "readers" and "actors"—the readers do the narrating while the others act out the story.

Dance in the Sky

Some birds, such as hummingbirds, have great maneuverability. Others, such as eagles and hawks, have perfected the art of soaring; almost all birds do some form of gliding. Birds glide when they use air currents and gravity to move over short distances, as when they move from tree to tree or descend from a higher to a lower altitude. Gliding requires little effort on the birds' part as they just extend their wings and allow the air current to carry them. Soaring, on the other hand, can be done over long distances but is limited to a rising current. When birds glide, they move in a downward direction and continue getting lower until they reach their destination. When birds soar, they move either upward or straight riding a current with little or no flapping of their wings.

Primary Objective

Children will observe and imitate different ways birds fly.

Materials

Bird cutouts
Bird puppet or stuffed animal or cutout of a bird

What You Can Do

1. Call attention to the movements of birds. Ask the children to think of some words to describe how the birds move. Are they hopping, running, soaring, flapping their wings, going fast or slow, moving in a straight line, or making circles in the sky?

2. Briefly introduce the words *gliding* and *soaring,* and demonstrate the meaning of each using a puppet, stuffed animal, or cutout of a bird.

3. Give the children cutouts of birds and have them glide and soar from one place to another.

4. Encourage the children to share ideas about how the birds might feel, what they might see, and what they might hear as they glide and soar.

Additional Suggestions

- Invite the children to pretend to be birds and to imitate different ways in which birds move.

- Have the children dance with scarves as they imitate the movements of bees, butterflies, fish, and even some mammals, such as deer and dolphins.

- Display pictures of birds in flight.

Animal Yoga

Yoga is a practice that engages the body, mind, and spirit. Both adults and children can benefit from yoga. Yoga involves movement and poses, some of which are based on animals and other entities in nature. Popular yoga poses include cobra, eagle, tree, and mountain.

Primary Objective

Children will practice animal poses and make animal movements.

What You Can Do

1. Ask the children if they've ever seen a cat arch its back. Invite a volunteer to demonstrate what this looks like. Explain that cats sometimes arch their backs to stretch after taking a nap and that sometimes they arch their backs when they feel threatened.

2. Have the children pretend to be cats just waking up from naps. Have them arch their backs and stretch.

3. Invite the children to suggest other animals they could imitate with body motions. Give them time to demonstrate what each would look like.

Additional Suggestions

- Read a children's book about animals. Have the children imitate the movements of the animals in the book.

- Play a game of charades, letting the children take turns acting out the behavior of an animal while the other children guess what it is. The idea is to use actions only rather than words to represent the selected animal.

- Play a game of Simon Says by having the children move like different animals. Choose animals they are familiar with, such as snakes, deer, rabbits, and so on: "Simon says, 'Run like a deer.'" "Slither like a snake." "Simon says, 'Hop like a bunny.'"

Nature Collage

The textures, colors, and shapes of the natural world have inspired many works of art. Countless paintings, sketches, and sculptures represent select elements of nature. At times, natural materials are even incorporated into works of art. For this activity, children use natural materials to create a collage.

Primary Objective

Children will become more aware of the characteristics of natural materials by using them in an art project.

Materials

Natural materials, such as, leaves, grass, sticks, and pebbles
Playdough
Small containers, such as paper bags, baskets, or bowls

What You Can Do

1. Give each child a small container for collecting natural materials. Go outside and collect a variety of small items. Remind the children not to harm plants or the homes of animals as they collect their materials.

2. Tell the children they will be using the natural items to make a collage. Explain the meaning of *collage*—art made by using different materials to form an arrangement.

3. Give each child some playdough. Tell them to shape the playdough any way they want to make a base for arranging their natural materials into a collage. Demonstrate different ideas for how they might want to shape the playdough—one flat piece, several balls, one mound, and so on.

4. Have the children press some of their natural items into the playdough base.

Additional Suggestions

- Have the children work together to make one large nature collage.

- Make nature collages based on a theme, such as parts of plants, things that are green, or things that are found in a forest.

- Use paper and glue instead of playdough to hold natural materials in place for the collage.

Name in Nature

There are many ways to integrate nature and literacy, and some can be done without paper, pencil, or books. One way that makes literacy very personal for young children is to have them use natural materials to write their names.

Primary Objective

Children will become more familiar with the beauty and characteristics of natural materials by using them to spell their names.

Materials

Natural materials, such as leaves, flowers, and pebbles

What You Can Do

1. Gather some leaves, flowers, pebbles, and other small natural materials.

2. Have the children spell their names by shaping these natural materials into letters. This might be done on a clear piece of ground, on a tabletop, or on a large sheet of paper or cardboard.

Additional Suggestions

- Make nameplates by using glue to outline each letter of a child's name on a sheet of paper. Have the children choose natural materials to place over the glue.

- Have children use a stick to write their name in mud or wet sand.

Nature's Paints

A variety of plant parts can be used to paint a picture. Blades of grass, flower petals, berries, and a variety of leaves can be squished to make natural colors. Of course, in working with younger children, you'll need to be careful to avoid poisonous plants.

Primary Objective

Children will become more familiar with the beauty and characteristics of natural materials by using them to paint a picture.

Materials

A variety of plant parts, such as leaves, flower petals, seed pods, and stems

What You Can Do

1. Gather some grass, flower petals, leaves, seed pods, and other plant parts.

2. Rub some grass across a sheet of paper to show the children how they can use plants to create colors to paint with.

3. Encourage the children to experiment with other plant parts to make markings on paper.

4. Once the children are familiar with how to squish the plant material to get the color out, encourage them to paint a picture.

Additional Suggestions

• Make an art gallery display of children's paintings.

• Cover a table top with a large sheet of paper. Encourage the children to work together using natural materials to create a picture of a forest or a garden.

• Have children gather their own natural materials from the yard. Remind them to be respectful of animals' homes and to be gentle with plants.

To Tell a Story

Pretend play often involves telling a story. The story might be about what adults do at home, at work, or for recreation. Many children will role play such activities as cooking, gardening, camping, fishing, driving cars, and working in a store or restaurant. With some adult guidance (if needed), these role-play scenarios can become dramatic performances. To strengthen children's connection with nature, you can encourage the performance of nature-related stories developed with the children.

Primary Objective

Children will participate in a dramatic performance of a nature-related story they develop.

What You Can Do

1. Choose a nature-related theme children can identify with, such as a bird with a broken wing or a duckling that gets separated from its mother.

2. Ask the children for ideas for a story built around this theme.

3. Explain that most stories have a beginning, a middle, and an end. Work with the children to decide what happens at the beginning, the middle, and the end of the story you're developing.

4. Identify with the children what characters should be in the story and what the setting should be.

5. Have the children suggest what props they could use in acting out this story, and then work with them in making and/or collecting these props.

6. Have the children perform the play based on the story they developed.

Additional Suggestion

Work with the children on how to use body language to dramatize different emotions. Encourage them to show how different animals might express such emotions as fear, excitement, anger, joy, and so on.

Take It Outside

While we often think of literacy and art in terms of indoor activities, there are many reasons to take them outdoors. Direct access to nature can be quite motivating and effective in helping children develop language and literacy-related skills and an appreciation of beauty. Nature is rich in sensory stimulation and readily excites the interest and imaginations of young children. Following are some suggestions for capitalizing on all that nature has to offer.

- **Establish an outdoor literacy and art center.** Start by selecting an appropriate location where children can sit to read, write, draw, and listen to stories and poems read aloud. Then add some interesting literacy- and art-related props. Include a variety of books—both fiction and nonfiction—and other types of reading materials, such as maps, brochures, and seed catalogues. At least some of the pictures and text should relate to what children are likely to see and experience in the outdoor setting, such as trees, soil, crickets, ants, birds, and sky. For promoting both literacy and art, provide materials for writing and drawing, such as paint, sculpting clay, chalk, and glue. Of course, the children will need a table or other suitable surface for working on their writing and art projects.

- **Take story time outdoors.** Identify a special gathering place that is conducive to listening and discussing where you and the children can share stories and poems. While you can share books of all kinds outdoors, find some that focus on the natural world and what children can see and experience in the outdoor setting.

- **Establish an outdoor performance area.** For this, you might provide an actual platform as a stage, but any designated area, such as a large circle of stones, will also work. Encourage the children to use this area to act out stories. They may choose to act out popular children's books or stories they have created themselves. Props can be made using materials from the literacy and art center.

Epilogue

· ·

Great teachers are reflective and intentional. They have a philosophy about education and use it to guide their practice. They care about children and the world in which we live. They've come to their own conclusions about the real purpose of education and remain focused on what they know to be in the best interests of children and the betterment of society.

Some people say that the purpose of education is to prepare students for success in college and careers and to help our country and communities compete successfully in the global economy. Others, however, feel differently. Liberty Hyde Bailey, a pioneer in the science of horticulture, wrote in *The Outlook to Nature* that "Sensitiveness to life is the highest product of education." But education today seems to be taking an entirely different direction. The focus is more on acquiring a predetermined set of facts and skills than on developing dispositions relating to "sensitiveness to life."

Competencies and assessments may lead to a more efficient educational system, but will they generate enthusiasm for life and learning? Will they help students become more compassionate and caring? Will they promote a more peaceful society? Will they promote a sustainable natural environment? These are questions we should be asking as we plan educational activities and experiences for students of all ages.

But what we do at the early childhood level holds special significance, as experiences during the early years play a critical role in shaping lifelong attitudes, values, and patterns of behavior. Connecting children with the rhythm of nature is one way to make the education of young children more meaningful for them and for the larger community. Such connections foster caring and compassion and can attune children to what is true, right, and lasting in this world. Children with strong connections to nature realize that the resources of the planet are limited and seek ways to live more sustainably.

In *The Sense of Wonder*, Rachel Carson explains how nature and the wonder it instills can serve "as an unfailing antidote against the boredom and disenchantments of later years, the sterile preoccupation with things that are artificial, the alienation from the sources of our strength."

It's unfortunate that some of us, as adults, no longer relate to nature as a source of wonder and excitement. While enchantment with the natural world may have been very much alive during our own childhood years, this way of knowing the world may have dimmed or even extinguished as we have gotten older. Young children, however, still have the chance to experience the world as a source of wonder and excitement. Let's give them that chance.

Glossary

. . . .

Aesthetic: concerned with beauty or the appreciation of beauty

Affective: relating to emotions

Affective domain: an area of development which includes feelings, motivation, attitudes, perceptions, and values

Affordance: quality or property of an object or environment that defines its possible uses

Aquatic: relating to water

Biophilia: instinctive bond between human beings and other living systems; innate affinity for other life forms

Coconstruction: working together to interpret and understand written or oral communication

Conservation: in math, the idea that the arrangement of a group of objects does not affect the quantity of the objects

Constructivism: a learning theory based on the idea that humans generate or build knowledge and meaning from their interactions with the world around them

Deciduous: in reference to a tree or shrub, shedding leaves annually

Dormant: in reference to a plant or animal, having normal physical functions suspended or slowed down for a period of time

Ecological autobiography: an autobiography focusing on one's experiences and relationship with the natural world

Ecological identity: how people view themselves in relationship to the natural world

Ecological perspective taking: being aware of how things in nature are affected by situations and events

Enchantment factor: an element or feature that contributes to the pleasantness or attraction of a place

Environmental literacy: the capacity to perceive and interpret the relative health of the natural world and to take appropriate action to maintain, restore, or improve the health of the environment

Environmental stewardship: responsible use and protection of the natural environment

Estivation: prolonged dormancy of an animal during a hot or dry period

Existential intelligence: a way of knowing that focuses on the meaning of existence

Extinction of experience: the loss of experience with certain elements of the natural world due to the loss of those elements

Forest kindergarten/forest school: an educational program for young children where students spend all or most of their school day outdoors

Habitat: the natural home or environment of an animal or plant

Hibernation: state of inactivity or dormancy over a period of time, usually during the winter, as a way of adapting to the cold weather and scarcity of food

Hypothesis: a proposed explanation based on evidence; a guess based on what is observed or known

Intentionality: ability to act with purpose

Intuition: direct perception of truth or fact; knowing in a way that is independent of reasoning

Kinesthetic sense: the sense of body position and movement of body parts in relation to each other

Narration: in reference to a teaching technique with young children, the act of describing or narrating what children are doing and/or experiencing

Native animal: an animal that is an original or indigenous inhabitant

Natural play space: a space intentionally designed to include natural features for play and active exploration

Naturalistic intelligence: the ability to recognize patterns and relationships in nature

Nature deficit disorder: stunted or diminished academic and developmental growth due to lack of routine contact with nature

Nature journal: a type of notebook used to record nature-related observations, experiences, and insights

Nature play: a type of play involving active engagement with nature

Nature preschool: a nature-focused early childhood program

Nocturnal: active at night

Open-ended activities: activities with no preset agenda, allowing children to determine the type and direction of the activities

Open-ended questions: questions with no right or wrong answers

Organism: an individual living thing

Philosophical: focusing on the fundamental nature or meaning of a concept or belief

Place-based education (PBE): an approach to education engaging students with the actual environment they are learning about

Place-based stories: stories using local settings and local characters; the characters may be people, animals, plants, and other parts of the local environment

Play partner: an adult who supports and facilitates a child's play in nondirective ways

Play unit: a single, designated area containing materials for play

Pronature book: a book with accurate information and/or positive messages about the natural world

Proprioceptive sense: the sense that detects one's own bodily position

Sense of place: a combination of features that makes a place special and unique; involves the human experience in a landscape

Sciencing: a slang term for active scientific exploration engaging both hands-on and minds-on inquiry

Scientific inquiry: activities through which students develop knowledge and understanding of scientific ideas in an active process of exploration

Shared sustained thinking (SST): two or more individuals working together to solve a problem or clarify a concept; the individuals involved contribute to the thinking in a serious, extended way

Somatosensory sense: the sense that detects pain, pressure, and temperature

Sustainable: capable of being maintained at a certain level

Transformability: the ability to change in a considerable way

Vestibular sense: the sense of body orientation with respect to gravity

Walking ropes: used to assist someone who has mobility challenges, including individuals with visual impairments

References

Bailey, Liberty Hyde. 1915. *The Outlook to Nature*. New York: Macmillan.

Blair, Dorothy. 2009. "The Child in the Garden: An Evaluative Review of the Benefits of School Gardening." *Journal of Environmental Education* 40(2): 15–38.

Carson, Rachel. 1956. *The Sense of Wonder*. New York: Harper and Row.

Environmental Education Council of Ohio. 2015. Environmental Education Council of Ohio, accessed December 21, 2015. Lancaster, OH: EECO. https://eeco.wildapricot.org

Frost, Joe, Sue Wortham, and Stuart Reifel. 2011. *Play and Child Development*. 4th edition. Boston: Pearson.

Gardner, Howard. 1983. *Frames of Mind: The Theory of Multiple Intelligences*. New York: Basic Books.

Gardner, Howard. 1999. *Intelligence Reframed: Multiple Intelligences for the 21st Century*. New York: Basic Books.

Gardner, Howard. 2006. *Multiple Intelligences: New Horizons in Theory and Practice*. New York: Basic Books.

Guiteras, Susan Talbott. n.d. "Ecological Autobiography" (unpublished manuscript).

Kriesberg, Daniel. 1999. *A Sense of Place: Teaching Children about the Environment with Picture Books*. Englewood, CO: Teacher Ideas Press.

Louv, Richard. 2008. *Last Child in the Woods: Saving Our Children from Nature-Deficit Disorder*. Chapel Hill, NC: Algonquin.

Louv, Richard. 2012. *The Nature Principle: Reconnecting with Life in a Virtual Age.* Chapel Hill, NC: Algonquin.

MacMillan, Meredith. 2008. "Books for Young Children about Nature." *Beyond the Journal:* Young Children *on the Web.* http://www.naeyc.org/files/yc/file/200801/BTJRecommendedNatureBooks.pdf

Moore, Robin, and Allen Cooper. 2014. *Nature Play and Learning Places: Creating and Managing Places Where Children Engage with Nature.* Raleigh, NC: Natural Learning Initiative and Reston, VA: National Wildlife Federation.

Nature Action Collaborative for Children. 2015. "Universal Principles for Connecting Children with Nature," accessed December 21, 2015. http://www.worldforumfoundation.org/wf/nacc/ibm/pdf/universal_princ_dvd_english.pdf

North American Association for Environmental Education. 2010. *Early Childhood Environmental Education Programs: Guidelines for Excellence.* Washington, DC: NAAEE. http://resources.spaces3.com/c518d93d-d91c-4358-ae5e-b09d493af3f4.pdf

O'Keeffe, Georgia. 1939. "About Myself." Georgia O'Keeffe: Exhibition of Oils and Pastels. An American Place Gallery, New York. n.p.

Pyle, Robert. 1993. *The Thunder Tree: Lessons from an Urban Wildland.* New York: Houghton Mifflin.

Taylor, Andrea, and Frances Kuo. 2006. "Is Contact with Nature Important for Healthy Child Development? State of the Evidence." In *Children and Their Environments: Learning, Using and Designing Spaces.* Cambridge, UK: Cambridge University Press.

Whitman, Walt. 1867. *Leaves of Grass.* 4th edition. New York: William Chapin.

Resources

. . . .

Acorn Naturalists

http://www.acornnaturalists.com

An excellent resource for animal puppets and other informational materials to add to your nature-related library.

Children and Nature Network

http://www.childrenandnature.org

An organization supporting the movement to reconnect children with nature, through information sharing and broad-based collaboration.

Dimensions Foundation

http://dimensionsfoundation.org

An organization conducting research and working with others in investigating how children's connections with the natural world can affect their holistic development. The Dimensions Foundation collaborates with the Arbor Day Foundation in providing educational opportunities through the national Nature Explore Program.

Gardening with Children

http://eartheasy.com/grow_gardening_children.htm

A website devoted to providing solutions for a sustainable environment, focusing on gardening with children.

Green Hearts Institute for Nature in Childhood

http://www.greenheartsinc.org

A nonprofit conservation organization dedicated to restoring and strengthening the bonds between children and nature. The work of this organization includes advocating for and providing consulting assistance to organizations interested in creating or expanding opportunities for nature play.

Kids Gardening

http://www.kidsgardening.org

A resource of the National Gardening Association, focusing on gardening with children. This organization provides grants, curricula, and lesson plans; ideas for family gardening; and links to other resources for gardening with kids.

Natural Learning Initiative

http://www.naturalearning.org

A research and professional-development unit at the College of Design, North Carolina State University, focusing on the importance of the natural environment in the daily experience of all children. The work includes environmental design, action research, education, and dissemination of information.

Natural Start Alliance

http://naturalstart.org

A coalition of educators, parents, organizations, and others working to help young children connect with nature and care for the environment. This alliance is a project of the NAAEE.

Nature Action Collaborative for Children

http://www.worldforumfoundation.org/working-groups/nature

A project of the World Forum Foundation, focusing on developmentally appropriate nature education for young children. The work includes disseminating information and providing professional-development opportunities.

Nature Explore

http://www.natureexplore.org

A program providing research-based outdoor classroom-design services, educator workshops, and natural products.

Nature Play and Learning Places: Creating and Managing Places Where Children Engage with Nature

http://natureplayandlearning.org

A set of guidelines published by the Natural Learning Initiative and the National Wildlife Federation, for developing nature spaces in the everyday environments of children, youth, and families.

Nature Songs

http://www.naturesongs.com

A reference library of common songs that you may hear in nature.

NatureStart Early Childhood Initiative and Professional Development Program

http://www.czs.org/NatureStart.aspx

An early childhood initiative and professional-development program of the Chicago Zoological Society, using children's innate curiosity about the natural world as a way to foster learning. NatureStart provides nature-play training for education professionals at museums, zoos, aquariums, and nature centers.

North American Association for Environmental Education (NAAEE)

The NAAEE publishes a variety of resources for educators:

Early Childhood Environmental Education Programs: Guidelines for Excellence

http://www.naaee.net/publications

A document published as part of the National Project for Excellence in Environmental Education. It presents key characteristics related to quality in early childhood environmental education programs.

Early Childhood Environmental Education Rating Scale

http://www.naaee.net/sites/default/files/publications/ECEERS.pdf

A formative evaluation tool to help programs improve nature education for young children. The content is based on the *Early Childhood Environmental Education Programs: Guidelines for Excellence* document.

International Journal of Early Childhood Environmental Education

http://www.naaee.net/publications/IJECEE

A scholarly journal focusing on topics relevant to environmental education at the early childhood level.

Recommended Children's Books

Allen, Judy. 2002. *Are You a Snail?* London: Kingfisher.

Baillie, Marilyn. 2003. *Amazing Things Animals Do.* Toronto: Maple Tree.

Baker, Jeannie. 2003. *Home in the Sky.* London: Walker.

Bancroft, Henrietta. 1997. *Animals in Winter.* New York: HarperCollins.

Baylor, Byrd. 1974. *Everybody Needs a Rock.* New York: Atheneum.

Baylor, Byrd, and Peter Parnall. 1978. *The Other Way to Listen.* New York: Simon and Schuster.

Brown, Marcia. 1947. *Stone Soup.* New York: Simon and Schuster.

Bunting, Eve. 1994. *Flower Garden.* Orlando, FL: Harcourt.

Carle, Eric. 1994. *The Very Hungry Caterpillar.* New York: Philomel.

Carle, Eric. 1999. *The Grouchy Ladybug.* New York: HarperFestival.

Carle, Eric. 2005. *My Very First Book of Shapes.* New York: Philomel.

Christian, Peggy. 2000. *If You Find a Rock.* Orlando, FL: Harcourt.

Davies, Jacqueline. 2004. *The Boy Who Drew Birds: A Story of John James Audubon.* New York: Houghton Mifflin.

Fisher, Aileen. 1980. *Anybody Home?* New York: Harper and Row.

Fredericks, Anthony. 2001. *Under One Rock: Bugs, Slugs, and Other Ughs*. Nevada City, CA: Dawn.

Ganeri, Anita. 2005. *Hibernation*. Portsmouth, NH: Heinemann.

Giogas, Valarie. 2007. *In My Backyard*. Mount Pleasant, SC: Sylvan Dell.

Hall, Margaret. 2006. *Hibernation*. North Mankato, MN: Capstone.

Hamanaka, Sheila. 1994. *All the Colors of the Earth*. New York: William Morrow.

Hickman, Pamela. 2005. *Animals Hibernating: How Animals Survive Extreme Conditions*. Toronto: Kids Can Press.

Hoban, Tana. 1998. *More, Fewer, Less*. New York: Greenwillow.

Hoberman, Mary Ann. 1978. *A House Is a House for Me*. New York.

Kalman, Bobbie. 2007. *Is It Big or Small?* New York: Crabtree.

Martin, Bill, Jr., and Michael Sampson. 2006. *I Love Our Earth*. Watertown, MA: Charlesbridge.

Mazer, Anne. 1991. *The Salamander Room*. New York: Dragonfly.

Parnall, Peter. 1991. *The Rock*. New York: Atheneum.

Penny, Malcolm. 2004. *Hidden Hibernators*. Portsmouth, NH: Heinemann.

Pluckrose, Henry Arthur. 1995. *Sorting*. New York: Watts.

Ruurs, Margriet. 2007. *In My Backyard*. Plattsburg, NY: Tundra.

Salas, Laura Purdie. 2006. *Do Polar Bears Snooze in Hollow Trees? A Book about Animal Hibernation*. North Mankato, MN: Capstone.

Seuss, Dr. 1973. *The Shape of Me and Other Stuff*. New York: Random House.

Showers, Paul. 1993. *The Listening Walk*. New York: HarperCollins.

Silverstein, Shel. 1964. *A Giraffe and a Half*. New York: HarperCollins.

Silverstein, Shel. 1964. *The Giving Tree*. Chicago, IL: Evil Eye Music.

Steffora, Tracey. 2011. *Sorting at the Market*. Portsmouth, NH: Heinemann.

Teckentrup, Britta. 2013. *Big and Small*. Cambridge, MA: Barefoot.

Udry, Janice May. 1987. *A Tree Is Nice*. New York: HarperCollins.

Wildsmith, Brian. 1981. *Animal Homes*. Kettering, Northamptonshire, UK: Oxford University Press.

Winter, Jeanette. 2011. *The Watcher: Jane Goodall's Life with the Chimps*. New York: Schwartz and Wade.

Index

E

early childhood environmental education (ECEE), 9
ecological perspective taking, 47–51
ecological self (identity), 28–30
emotions, 10
environmental education, defined, 26–27
Environmental Education Council of Ohio, 26
environmental yards, 24
experimentation, 98
exploration, 71–97
exploratory play, 34
Exploring More, 124–125
extinction of experience, 14

F

fantasy play, 34
Florida Atlantic University, 25
focus attention, 64–65
forest kindergartens (schools), 24
fractions, concept of, 130–131
Frames of Mind: The Theory of Multiple Intelligences (Gardner), 7, 8
Froebel, F., 27
Frost, J., 33

G

games with rules, 35
gardening, 20–21, 24, 38–39, 102–105
Gardening with Children, 181
Gardner, H., 7, 8
Green Hearts Institute for Nature in Childhood, 181–182
Growing Like a Tree, 50–51
Growing Peas, 104–105
Guiteras, S. T., 28–30

H

Hibernation, 92–93

I

Icy Places, 76–77
indoor/outdoor connections
    animals, 110–111, 112–113

P

Q

R

S

T

U

W